"sweets to the sweet"

—WILLIAM SHAKESPEARE, *Hamlet*

the candy cookbook

✤

Recipes for spectacular

TRUFFLES, BRITTLES, TOFFEES, CHOCOLATES, AND MORE

by CAROLE BLOOM

Illustrations by DAN HUBIG

CHRONICLE BOOKS

SAN FRANCISCO

Printed in Hong Kong.

Library of Congress Cataloging-in-Publication Data:
Bloom, Carole.
    The candy cookbook : recipes for spectacular truffles, brittles, toffees,
chocolates, and more / by Carole Bloom ; illustrations by Dan Hubig.
        p.   cm.
    Includes index.
    ISBN 0-8118-0519-0
    1.   Candy.   I.   Title.
TX791.B647   1995
641.8'53—dc20   94-43509
                                                            CIP
Design: Jill Jacobson.

Distributed in Canada by Raincoast Books,
    8680 Cambie Street, Vancouver, B.C. V6P 6M9

10   9   8   7   6   5   4   3   2   1

Chronicle Books
275 Fifth Street
San Francisco, CA 94103

Dedicated with love to

MY HUSBAND, JERRY, MY PREMIER TASTER

⚜

OUR CAT, POOKER, WHO SLEEPS THROUGH EVERYTHING

⚜

MY MOTHER, FLORENCE, WHO LOVES MY CANDIES

⚜

MY BROTHER MICHAEL, MY FIRST FOOD FAN AND A CHAMPION CANDY EATER

⚜

AND MY NEPHEWS BRANDON AND ETHAN,
WHO ARE SWEET AS CAN BE WITHOUT EATING CANDY,
WHICH THEY LOVE TO DO

Acknowledgments

My husband, Jerry Olivas, is truly my hero. He is always ready to help me, whether it's brainstorming about recipes, tasting them, cleaning up the kitchen when it is full of chocolate, fine-tuning a sentence, fixing a computer glitch, holding my hand, or just making me laugh. His constant enthusiastic support keeps me going.

✤

Sincere thanks to my agent, Jane Dystel, for her sage advice and counsel and for helping me to fulfill my goals. Every author should be so fortunate.

✤

Thanks are due to my good friend Jan Bos Meyers for sharing many recipe suggestions and ideas.

✤

And to my personal support team of colleagues Betz Collins, Kitty Morse, and Lily Loh, who always cheer me on and gladly volunteer as taste-testers.

✤

Thanks to Dan Hubig for his elegant artwork and to Bill LeBlond and Leslie Jonath of Chronicle Books, who so carefully guided my manuscript through the publishing process.

contents

the joy of candy

CANDY IS MY PASSION. I love to make it, and I love to eat it. I can eat it any time of the day or night. I am definitely not alone on the eating part. Almost everyone I know loves good candy. However, most people have to rely on store-bought candy. This book shows you how to make candy easily at home. Candy that is much, much better than store-bought.

Homemade candy is better because, for one thing, the ingredients used are fresher and purer. Also, no preservatives or stabilizers are used and homemade candy does not sit on the shelf, or in a case, for weeks. Homemade candy is too irresistible to last for very long.

The recipes in this book are very simple to follow. Each recipe lists the ingredients in the order they are used, followed by short, easy-to-understand, step-by-step instructions. All the recipes are for small quantities; most can be doubled without any problem. Much of what you need in the way of equipment, utensils, and ingredients is probably already in your kitchen.

Here are some tips that will help you get started with your candy making. The sooner you get started, the sooner you will be experiencing the joy of making and eating great candies.

✤　　　Read each recipe through before beginning so you know what needs to be done. For example, some recipes have you make component parts first, which you return to later to finish the candy. Others have you move more quickly when you come to a certain point or temperature. By reading the recipe in advance you will feel more comfortable when you are making it.

✤　　　Have all your ingredients measured out and ready for each recipe. By doing this you make sure that you have included all the necessary ingredients. When measuring dry ingredients use the nested sets of measuring cups. Whether you scoop the measuring cup into the ingredient or spoon the ingredient into the cup, make sure to sweep off the top so that it is level with the top edge of the cup. For liquid measures use the measuring cups with pour spouts and read the lines at eye level. It is especially important in candy making to be exact, so measure all ingredients accurately.

✤　　　Make sure that you have all the necessary utensils and equipment before you begin. Set these out so that they are within easy reach.

✤　　　Don't rush through a recipe. Go slowly and double-check yourself. You can start with any recipe; recipes that require only a few ingredients and have just a few steps are a good way to begin. You will soon see how easy it is to make super candy in a short time with very little effort.

Happy candy making!

—Carole Bloom

terrific truffles

Dark Chocolate Truffles

CHOCOLATE TRUFFLES ARE A WHIMSICAL INTERPRETATION OF THE TRUFFLES
THAT GROW ON THE ROOTS OF OAK TREES IN FRANCE AND ITALY. MANY PEOPLE
CONSIDER THEM TO BE THE ULTIMATE CHOCOLATE CONFECTION.

9 ounces bittersweet or semisweet chocolate, finely chopped
⅔ cup whipping cream
1 teaspoon vanilla extract
1½ tablespoons dark rum or cognac
2 to 3 tablespoons unsweetened Dutch process cocoa powder, in a dredger
1 pound bittersweet or semisweet chocolate, finely chopped, for tempering (page 96)

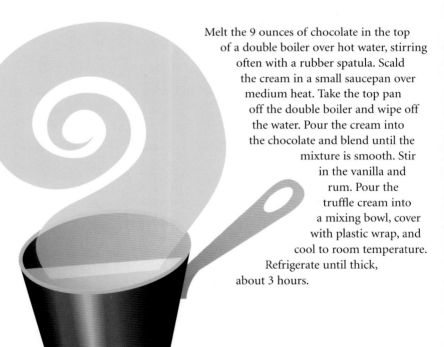

Melt the 9 ounces of chocolate in the top
of a double boiler over hot water, stirring
often with a rubber spatula. Scald
the cream in a small saucepan over
medium heat. Take the top pan
off the double boiler and wipe off
the water. Pour the cream into
the chocolate and blend until the
mixture is smooth. Stir
in the vanilla and
rum. Pour the
truffle cream into
a mixing bowl, cover
with plastic wrap, and
cool to room temperature.
Refrigerate until thick,
about 3 hours.

Line a baking sheet with wax paper. Using a 12-inch pastry bag fitted with a ½-inch round tip, pipe 1-inch diameter mounds of the truffle cream onto the baking sheet. Cover with plastic wrap and chill in the freezer until firm, about 2 hours.

To form truffle centers, sprinkle cocoa powder on your hands and shape the mounds into balls. Cover and chill in the freezer until firm, about 2 hours.

Line another baking sheet with wax paper. Melt and temper the chocolate. Using a fork or dipping tool, dip each truffle center in the chocolate and shake off the excess as it is lifted out. Place the truffles on the baking sheet and refrigerate for 15 minutes, to set the chocolate.

Place each truffle in a paper candy cup and serve at room temperature. Store the truffles between layers of wax paper in an airtight container wrapped with aluminum foil in the refrigerator for up to 3 weeks or in the freezer for up to 2 months.

Makes 36 truffles

Variation:

Nut Truffles

Add ½ cup finely ground toasted nuts, such as hazelnuts, to the truffle cream after adding the vanilla. Replace the rum with Frangelico or a liqueur that complements the nuts. After dipping a truffle in the tempered chocolate, sprinkle a pinch of finely ground toasted nuts on the top before the chocolate sets up.

Black Forest Truffles

MY INSPIRATION FOR THESE TRUFFLES CAME FROM THE FAMOUS,
CLASSIC BLACK FOREST CHERRY TORTE WITH ITS COMBINATION
OF DARK CHOCOLATE, CREAM, CHERRIES, AND KIRSCHWASSER.

9 ounces bittersweet or semisweet chocolate, finely chopped
⅔ cup whipping cream
2 tablespoons plus 2 teaspoons kirschwasser
½ cup finely chopped dried cherries
3 to 4 tablespoons unsweetened Dutch process cocoa powder, in a dredger
1 pound bittersweet or semisweet chocolate, finely chopped, for tempering (page 96)
40 slivers dried cherries

Melt the 9 ounces of chocolate in the top of a double boiler over hot water, stirring often with a rubber spatula. Scald the cream in a small saucepan over medium heat. Take the top pan off the double boiler and wipe off the water. Pour the cream into the chocolate and blend until the mixture is smooth. Stir in the kirschwasser and the chopped dried cherries. Pour the truffle cream into a mixing bowl, cover with plastic wrap, and cool to room temperature. Refrigerate until thick, about 3 hours.

Line a baking sheet with wax paper. Using a 12-inch pastry bag fitted with a ¾-inch round tip, pipe 1¼-inch diameter mounds of the truffle cream onto the baking sheet. Cover with plastic wrap and chill in the freezer until firm, about 2 hours.

To form truffle centers, sprinkle some of the cocoa powder on your hands and shape the mounds into balls. Cover and chill in the freezer until firm, about 2 hours.

Line another baking sheet with wax paper. Melt and temper the chocolate. Using a fork or dipping tool, dip each truffle center in the chocolate, shaking off the excess as it is lifted out. Place the truffle on the baking sheet and lightly dust the top with some of the remaining cocoa powder, then center a sliver of dried cherry on top before the chocolate firms up. Refrigerate the truffles for 15 minutes, to set the chocolate.

Place each truffle in a paper candy cup and serve at room temperature. Store the truffles between layers of wax paper in an airtight container wrapped with aluminum foil in the refrigerator for up to 3 weeks or in the freezer for up to 2 months.

Makes 40 truffles

Port Truffles

PORT IS A DELICIOUS ACCOMPANIMENT
TO CHOCOLATE. I THOUGHT IT WOULD TASTE GREAT
BLENDED WITH THE CHOCOLATE, INSTEAD OF BEING
DRUNK ON THE SIDE. SERVE THESE TRUFFLES WITH
AFTER-DINNER COFFEE OR ACCOMPANIED WITH
MORE PORT. BE SURE TO USE THE SAME PORT
FOR MAKING THE TRUFFLES THAT
YOU ARE GOING TO DRINK.

8 ounces bittersweet or semisweet
chocolate, finely chopped
½ cup whipping cream
3 tablespoons port
½ cup unsweetened Dutch process
cocoa powder

Melt the chocolate in the top of a double boiler over hot water, stirring often with a rubber spatula. Scald the cream in a small saucepan over medium heat. Take the top pan off the double boiler and wipe off the water. Pour the cream into the chocolate and blend until the mixture is smooth. Stir in the port. Pour the truffle cream into a mixing bowl, cover with plastic wrap, and cool to room temperature. Refrigerate until thick, about 3 hours.

Line a baking sheet with wax paper. Using a 12-inch pastry bag fitted with a ½-inch round tip, pipe ¾-inch diameter mounds of the truffle cream onto the baking sheet. Cover with plastic wrap and chill in the freezer until firm, about 2 hours.

No longer than 1 hour before serving, place 2 tablespoons of the cocoa powder in a dredger. Dust your hands with this cocoa powder and shape the mounds into balls. Place the remaining cocoa powder in a small bowl and roll the truffle centers in the cocoa powder to coat them completely. (If the truffles are rolled in cocoa powder more than 1 hour before serving, the cocoa will dissolve into them and they will need to be rolled in cocoa again.)

Place the truffles in paper candy cups and serve at room temperature. Store the truffles between layers of wax paper in an airtight container wrapped with aluminum foil in the refrigerator for up to 1 week or in the freezer for up to 1 month.

Makes 36 truffles

White Chocolate Citrus Truffles

LEMON AND ORANGE ZESTS ADD ZIP TO THESE WHITE CHOCOLATE TRUFFLES.
THE ZEST IS THE OUTER, COLORED RIND THAT CONTAINS THE FRUIT'S PERFUME
AND SWEET FLAVOR. A SLIVER OF CANDIED ORANGE OR LEMON PEEL
CROWNS EACH WHITE CHOCOLATE-DIPPED TRUFFLE.

1 lemon
1 orange
1 cup whipping cream
12 ounces white chocolate, finely chopped
2 to 3 tablespoons confectioners' sugar, in a dredger
1 pound white chocolate, finely chopped, for tempering (page 96)
42 slivers candied orange or lemon peel (page 94)

Use a citrus stripper to remove two ¾ x 2-inch strips of the zest from both the
lemon and orange. Scald the cream in a small saucepan over medium heat. Add the
lemon and orange strips. Remove the pan from the heat, cover, and infuse the mixture
for 30 minutes. Strain the cream into a small bowl.

Melt the 12 ounces of white chocolate in the top of a double boiler over hot water,
stirring often with a rubber spatula. Take the top pan off the double boiler and wipe
off the water. Pour the cream into the chocolate and blend until the mixture is smooth.
Pour the truffle cream into a mixing bowl, cover with plastic wrap, and cool to room
temperature. Refrigerate until thick, about 6 hours.

Place the truffle cream in the bowl of a stand mixer or in a mixing bowl. Using
the flat beater attachment or a hand-held mixer, beat at low speed until the mixture is
thick and holds soft peaks, about 1 minute. Be careful not to overbeat the chocolate
or it will become grainy.

Line a baking sheet with wax paper. Using a 12-inch pastry bag fitted with a ½-inch round tip, pipe 1-inch diameter mounds of the truffle cream onto the baking sheet. Cover with plastic wrap and chill in the freezer until firm, about 2 hours.

To form truffle centers, sprinkle confectioners' sugar on your hands and shape the mounds into balls. Cover and chill in the freezer until firm, about 2 hours.

Line another baking sheet with wax paper. Melt and temper the white chocolate. Using a fork or dipping tool, dip each truffle center in the chocolate, shaking off the excess as it is lifted out. Place the truffle on the baking sheet and center a sliver of candied orange or lemon peel on top before the chocolate firms up. Refrigerate the truffles for 15 minutes, to set the chocolate.

Place each truffle in a paper candy cup and serve at room temperature. Store the truffles between layers of wax paper in an airtight container wrapped with aluminum foil in the refrigerator for up to 3 weeks or in the freezer for up to 2 months.

Makes 42 truffles

Vanilla Truffles

THE RICH FLAVOR OF PURE VANILLA STRAIGHT FROM VANILLA BEANS PERVADES
THESE TRUFFLES. BE SURE TO BUY ONLY VANILLA BEANS THAT ARE PLUMP AND SOFT.
ITALIAN GALLIANO LIQUEUR, WHICH TASTES LIKE BOTH VANILLA AND ANISE,
ADDS A LIGHT SPICY TOUCH AND ENHANCES THE FLAVORS
OF BOTH THE VANILLA AND THE WHITE CHOCOLATE.

2 vanilla beans
⅓ cup whipping cream
8 ounces white chocolate, finely chopped
1 tablespoon Galliano or cognac
2 to 3 tablespoons confectioners' sugar, in a dredger
8 ounces white chocolate, finely chopped, for tempering (page 96)

Split the vanilla beans lengthwise and place them with the cream in a small saucepan. Scald the cream over medium heat. Remove the pan from the heat, cover, and infuse the mixture for 20 minutes. Using a small sharp knife scrape the vanilla seeds from the beans into the cream, discarding the beans. Warm the cream again over medium heat.

Melt the 8 ounces of white chocolate in the top of a double boiler over hot water, stirring often with a rubber spatula. Take the top pan off the double boiler and wipe off the water. Pour the cream into the chocolate and blend until the mixture is smooth. Stir in the Galliano. Pour the truffle cream into a mixing bowl, cover with plastic wrap, and cool to room temperature. Refrigerate until thick, 3 to 4 hours.

Line a baking sheet with wax paper. Using a 12-inch pastry bag fitted with a ½-inch round tip, pipe 1-inch diameter mounds of the truffle cream onto the baking sheet. Cover with plastic wrap and chill in the freezer until firm, about 2 hours.

To form truffle centers, sprinkle confectioners' sugar on your hands and shape the mounds into balls. Cover and chill in the freezer until firm, about 2 hours.

Line another baking sheet with wax paper. Melt and temper the white chocolate. Using a fork or dipping tool, dip each truffle center in the chocolate, shaking off the excess as it is lifted out. Place the truffle on the baking sheet. Refrigerate the truffles for 15 minutes, to set the chocolate.

Place each truffle in a paper candy cup and serve at room temperature. Store the truffles between layers of wax paper in an airtight container wrapped with aluminum foil in the refrigerator for up to 3 weeks or in the freezer for up to 2 months.

Makes 32 truffles

Cinnamon Truffles

CINNAMON IS USED BOTH INSIDE AND OUTSIDE THESE TRUFFLES.
IT IS COMBINED WITH THE TRUFFLE CREAM, ADDING ITS PIQUANT, SPICY FLAVOR
TO THE INSIDE, AND IT IS LIGHTLY DUSTED OVER THE OUTER CHOCOLATE COATING,
MAKING A SUPER COLOR CONTRAST AND GIVING A HINT OF WHAT'S INSIDE.

9 ounces bittersweet or semisweet chocolate, finely chopped
⅔ cup whipping cream
¼ teaspoon freshly grated nutmeg
1½ teaspoons ground cinnamon
1 teaspoon vanilla extract
2 to 3 tablespoons unsweetened Dutch process cocoa powder, in a dredger
10 ounces bittersweet or semisweet chocolate, finely chopped, for tempering (page 96)

Melt the 9 ounces of chocolate in the top of a double boiler over hot water, stirring often with a rubber spatula. Scald the cream in a small saucepan over medium heat. Take the top pan off the double boiler and wipe off the water. Pour the cream into the chocolate and blend until the mixture is smooth. Stir in the nutmeg and 1 teaspoon of the cinnamon and blend thoroughly. Pour the truffle cream into a mixing bowl, cover with plastic wrap, and cool to room temperature. Refrigerate until thick, 3 to 4 hours.

Line a baking sheet with wax paper. Using a 12-inch pastry bag fitted with a ½-inch round tip, pipe 1-inch diameter mounds of the truffle cream onto the baking sheet. Cover with plastic wrap and chill in the freezer until firm, about 2 hours.

To form truffle centers, sprinkle cocoa powder on your hands and shape the mounds into balls. Cover and chill the truffle centers in the freezer until firm, about 2 hours.

Line another baking sheet with wax paper. Melt and temper the chocolate. Using a fork or dipping tool, dip each truffle center in the chocolate, shaking off the excess as it is lifted out. Place the truffle on the baking sheet and sprinkle a pinch of the remaining ½ teaspoon ground cinnamon on top of each before the chocolate firms up. Refrigerate the truffles for 15 minutes, to set the chocolate.

Place each truffle in a paper candy cup and serve at room temperature. Store the truffles between layers of wax paper in an airtight container wrapped with aluminum foil in the refrigerator for up to 3 weeks or in the freezer for up to 2 months.

Makes 48 truffles

Caramel Chocolate Truffles

I LOVE THE WARM, TOASTY FLAVOR OF CARAMEL. IT IS SUPERB COMBINED WITH DARK CHOCOLATE. THESE TRUFFLES ARE ESPECIALLY GOOD WITH AFTER-DINNER COFFEE.

¼ cup granulated sugar
2 tablespoons water
½ teaspoon freshly squeezed lemon juice
¾ cup whipping cream
9 ounces bittersweet or semisweet chocolate, finely chopped
2 to 3 tablespoons unsweetened Dutch process cocoa powder, in a dredger
12 ounces bittersweet or semisweet chocolate, finely chopped, for tempering (page 96)

Combine the sugar, water, and lemon juice in a small heavy-bottomed saucepan. Cook over low heat for a few minutes, stirring with a wooden spoon to dissolve the sugar. Raise the heat to medium-high and bring to a boil. Brush down the sides of the pan with a pastry brush dipped in warm water to dissolve any sugar crystals. Cook the mixture until it begins to turn a light caramel color. Swirl the pan a few times and remove from the heat when it is a rich, medium-dark color. ·

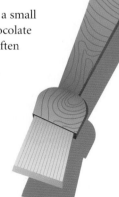

While the caramel is cooking, scald the cream in a small saucepan over medium heat. Melt the 9 ounces of chocolate in the top of a double boiler over hot water, stirring often with a rubber spatula.

Place the pan of caramel back over medium-low heat and slowly pour the hot cream into the caramel, stirring constantly with a long-handled wooden spoon. Cook the mixture, stirring constantly, until the caramel is completely dissolved.

Take the top pan off the double boiler and wipe off the water. Pour the cream into the chocolate and blend until the mixture is smooth. Pour the truffle cream into a mixing bowl, cover with plastic wrap, and cool to room temperature. Refrigerate until thick, 3 to 4 hours. Line a baking sheet with wax paper. Using a 12-inch pastry bag fitted with a ½-inch round tip, pipe 1-inch diameter mounds of the truffle cream onto the baking sheet. Cover with plastic wrap and chill in the freezer until firm, about 2 hours.

To form truffle centers, sprinkle cocoa powder on your hands and shape the mounds into balls. Cover and chill in the freezer until firm, about 2 hours.

Line another baking sheet with wax paper. Melt and temper the chocolate. Using a fork or dipping tool, dip each truffle center in the chocolate, shaking off the excess as it is lifted out. Place the truffles on the baking sheet. Refrigerate the truffles for 15 minutes, to set the chocolate.

Place each truffle in a paper candy cup and serve at room temperature. Store the truffles between layers of wax paper in an airtight container wrapped with aluminum foil in the refrigerator for up to 3 weeks or in the freezer for up to 2 months.

Makes 54 truffles

Tangerine Truffles

THE TANG OF TANGERINE IS JOINED WITH DARK CHOCOLATE IN THESE TRUFFLES.
A SLIVER OF CANDIED TANGERINE PEEL ADORNS THE TOP.

2 tangerines
½ cup whipping cream
8 ounces bittersweet or semisweet chocolate, finely chopped
1 tablespoon Mandarine Napoleon, Grand Marnier, or cognac
2 to 3 tablespoons unsweetened Dutch process cocoa powder, in a dredger
10 ounces bittersweet or semisweet chocolate, finely chopped, for tempering (page 96)
36 slivers candied tangerine peel (page 94)

Use a citrus stripper to remove the zest of one of the tangerines in thick strips. Finely grate the zest of the remaining tangerine and set aside in a small bowl covered with plastic wrap. (Be careful not to grate any of the white pith under the zest.) Scald the cream in a small saucepan over medium heat. Add the tangerine strips. Remove the pan from the heat, cover, and infuse the mixture for 30 minutes. Strain the cream into a small bowl.

Melt the 8 ounces of chocolate in the top of a double boiler over hot water, stirring often with a rubber spatula. Take the top pan off the double boiler and wipe off the water. Pour the cream into the chocolate and blend until the mixture is smooth. Stir in the grated tangerine zest and the liqueur. Blend well. Pour the truffle cream into a mixing bowl, cover with plastic wrap, and cool to room temperature. Refrigerate until thick, 3 to 4 hours.

Line a baking sheet with wax paper. Using a 12-inch pastry bag fitted with a ½-inch round tip, pipe 1-inch diameter mounds of the truffle cream onto the baking sheet. Cover with plastic wrap and chill in the freezer until firm, about 2 hours.

To form truffle centers, sprinkle cocoa powder on your hands and shape the mounds into balls. Cover and chill in the freezer until firm, about 2 hours.

Line another baking sheet with wax paper. Melt and temper the chocolate. Using a fork or dipping tool, dip each truffle center in the chocolate, shaking off the excess as it is lifted out. Place the truffle on the baking sheet and center a sliver of candied tangerine peel on top before the chocolate firms up. Refrigerate the truffles for 15 minutes, to set the chocolate.

Place each truffle in a paper candy cup and serve at room temperature. Store the truffles between layers of wax paper in an airtight container wrapped with aluminum foil in the refrigerator for up to 3 weeks or in the freezer for up to 2 months.

Makes 36 truffles

Ginger Chocolate Truffles

THE SPICY FLAVOR OF GINGER BLENDS PERFECTLY WITH CHOCOLATE.
WHEN YOU BITE INTO ONE OF THESE TRUFFLES, A BURST OF FLAVOR FROM
THE GINGER LIQUEUR AND THE RICH TASTE OF DARK CHOCOLATE ARE YOUR REWARD.

9 ounces bittersweet or semisweet chocolate, finely chopped
⅔ cup whipping cream
2 tablespoons plus 2 teaspoons Canton
2 to 3 tablespoons unsweetened Dutch process cocoa powder, in a dredger
1 pound bittersweet or semisweet chocolate, finely chopped, for tempering
    (page 96)
48 slivers crystallized ginger

Melt the 9 ounces of chocolate in the top of a double boiler over hot water, stirring often with a rubber spatula. Scald the cream in a small saucepan over medium heat. Take the top pan off the double boiler and wipe off the water. Pour the cream into the chocolate and blend until the mixture is smooth. Stir in the Canton. Pour the truffle cream into a mixing bowl, cover with plastic wrap, and cool to room temperature. Refrigerate until thick, about 3 hours.

Line a baking sheet with wax paper. Using a 12-inch pastry bag fitted with a ½-inch round tip, pipe 1-inch diameter mounds of the truffle cream onto the baking sheet. Cover with plastic wrap and chill in the freezer until firm, about 2 hours.

To form truffle centers, sprinkle cocoa powder on your hands and shape the mounds into balls. Cover and chill in the freezer until firm, about 2 hours.

Line another baking sheet with wax paper. Melt and temper the chocolate. Using a fork or dipping tool, dip each truffle center in the chocolate, shaking off the excess as it is lifted out. Place the truffle on the baking sheet and center a sliver of crystallized ginger on the top before the chocolate firms up. Refrigerate the truffles for 15 minutes, to set the chocolate.

Place each truffle in a paper candy cup and serve at room temperature. Store the truffles between layers of wax paper in an airtight container wrapped with aluminum foil in the refrigerator for up to 3 weeks or in the freezer for up to 2 months.

Makes 48 truffles

White Chocolate-Hazelnut-Apricot Clusters

WHITE CHOCOLATE, TOASTED HAZELNUTS, AND SWEET DRIED APRICOTS
MAKE MOUTH-WATERING CLUSTERS. USE OTHER NUTS AND CANDIED
OR DRIED FRUITS TO MAKE OTHER DIFFERENT TASTING ONES.

8 ounces white chocolate, finely chopped
1 cup toasted and skinned hazelnuts, roughly chopped, chilled
1 cup roughly chopped dried apricots, at room temperature

Melt the chocolate in the top of a double boiler over hot water, stirring often with a rubber spatula. Take the double boiler off the burner, take off the top pan, and place it over a larger bowl with about 1 inch of cool water. Gently stir the chocolate to reduce the temperature to 92°F., about 10 minutes. Be careful not to allow any water to mix with the chocolate. To test if the chocolate is at the right temperature, use a chocolate or instant-read thermometer or place a dab below your lower lip. The chocolate should feel comfortable, not hot and not cold. When it reaches this temperature, replace the pan of chocolate over the pan of warm water.

Line a baking sheet with wax paper. Thoroughly mix the hazelnuts and dried apricots together in a bowl, then stir them into the chocolate, coating them completely. Using a spoon, form 1-inch diameter clusters and place them on the baking sheet. Place the baking sheet in the refrigerator for 15 minutes, to set the clusters.

Place the clusters in paper candy cups and serve at room temperature. Store the clusters between layers of wax paper in an airtight container wrapped with aluminum foil in the refrigerator for up to 3 weeks or in the freezer for up to 2 months.

Makes about 36 clusters

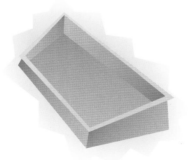

Miniature Peanut Butter Cups

PEANUT BUTTER AND CHOCOLATE ARE AN ALL-TIME FAVORITE FLAVOR COMBINATION.
MY VERSION OF THIS CLASSIC CANDY HAS A CREAMY CENTER LOCKED INSIDE
RICH BITTERSWEET CHOCOLATE. I PREFER TO USE LAURA SCUDDER'S
NATURAL BRAND OF PEANUT BUTTER.
MILK CHOCOLATE CAN BE USED IN PLACE OF THE DARK CHOCOLATE.

1 pound bittersweet or semisweet chocolate, finely chopped, for tempering (page 96)
¾ cup smooth peanut butter, at room temperature

Use 2 chocolate molds that each have twelve 1½-inch diameter fluted-edge cups.
Line the cups with paper candy cups. Prepare 3 parchment paper pastry bags (page 111).
Melt and temper the chocolate. Transfer half of the chocolate to one of the
parchment paper pastry bags. Fold down the top and snip off about ¼ inch at the tip.
Pipe chocolate into each cup, filling it about one third. Fill another parchment paper
pastry bag halfway with the peanut butter. Fold down the top and cut off about ¼ inch
at the tip. Carefully pipe peanut butter into the center of the chocolate in each cup,
filling it three quarters. Fill the remaining parchment paper pastry bag with the
remaining chocolate. Fold down the top and cut off ¼ inch at the tip. Pipe chocolate
into each cup, filling it to the top and covering the peanut butter filling. Gently tap
the molds against the countertop a few times to help the chocolate spread evenly in the
cup and release any air bubbles that would form holes in the chocolate when it is set.
Transfer the molds to a baking sheet and place the baking sheet on a flat surface in
the freezer for 20 minutes.
Remove the cups from the molds and serve at room temperature. Store the
peanut butter cups between layers of wax paper in an airtight container wrapped with
aluminum foil in the refrigerator for up to 3 weeks or in the freezer for up to 2 months.

Makes 24 cups

Jan's Frosted Almonds

MY GOOD FRIEND JAN MEYERS WAS GENEROUS ENOUGH TO SHARE HER RECIPE FOR
THESE DELICIOUS SUGAR-COATED ALMONDS. YOU CAN USE OTHER NUTS
AND OTHER LIQUEURS AS IN THE VARIATION AT THE END OF THE RECIPE.

¾ cup sugar
¼ cup amaretto
1½ cups whole unblanched almonds

Line a baking sheet with aluminum foil. Combine the sugar and amaretto in a
1½-quart heavy-bottomed saucepan. Cook the mixture over high heat until it reaches
238°F. on a candy thermometer, about 6 minutes. Using a damp pastry brush, wash
down the sides of the pan 2 times while the mixture is cooking, to prevent sugar
crystallization.

When the mixture is at the correct temperature, take the pan off of the heat and
immediately stir in the almonds, using a long-handled wooden spoon. Continue to stir
for another minute or two until the sugar syrup becomes cloudy. Turn the almonds out
onto the baking sheet, using the wooden spoon to spread them out. Leave the almonds
to cool completely, about 15 minutes. Using your fingers, separate the almonds into
individual nuts.

Serve the almonds at room temperature. Store them between layers of wax paper
in an airtight container at room temperature for up to 2 weeks.

Makes about 2½ cups nuts

yum   yum

Variation:

SUGARED HAZELNUTS
Replace the amaretto with ¼ cup
Frangelico and use 1½ cups whole
toasted and skinned hazelnuts in
place of the almonds.

Orange-Almond Clusters

DARK CHOCOLATE, CANDIED ORANGE PEEL, AND TOASTED ALMONDS ARE
THE ONLY INGREDIENTS IN THESE CANDIES. THEY ARE EASY TO MAKE AND
KEEP VERY WELL. BE CREATIVE AND INVENT NEW CLUSTERS BY USING
OTHER NUTS AND CANDIED OR DRIED FRUITS.

7 ounces bittersweet or semisweet chocolate, finely chopped
1 cup finely chopped candied orange peel, at room temperature (page 94)
1 cup toasted whole unblanched almonds, roughly chopped, chilled

Melt the chocolate in the top of a double boiler over hot water, stirring often with
a rubber spatula. Take the double boiler off the burner, take off the top pan, and place
it over a larger bowl with about 1 inch of cool water. Gently stir the chocolate to reduce
its temperature to 95°F., about 8 minutes. Be careful not to allow water to mix with
the chocolate. To test if the chocolate is at the right temperature, use a chocolate or
instant-read thermometer or place a dab below your lower lip. The chocolate should
feel comfortable, not hot and not cold. When it reaches this temperature, replace the
pan of chocolate over the pan of warm water.

Line a baking sheet with wax paper. Thoroughly mix the candied orange peel and
almonds together in a bowl, then stir them into the chocolate, coating them completely.
Using a spoon, form 1-inch diameter clusters and place them on the baking sheet. Place
the baking sheet in the refrigerator for 15 minutes, to set the clusters.

Place the clusters in paper candy cups and serve at room temperature. Store the
clusters between layers of wax paper in an airtight container wrapped in aluminum foil
in the refrigerator for up to 3 weeks or in the freezer for up to 2 months.

Makes about 36 clusters

Variations:

WHITE CHOCOLATE-ORANGE-ALMOND CLUSTERS
Replace the bittersweet chocolate with 8 ounces white chocolate.

ORANGE-PECAN CLUSTERS
Replace the almonds with toasted pecans.

CHERRY-ALMOND CLUSTERS
Replace the candied orange peel with 1 cup plus
1 tablespoon roughly chopped dried cherries.

STRAWBERRY-ALMOND CLUSTERS
Replace the candied orange peel with 1 cup plus
1 tablespoon roughly chopped dried strawberries.

BLUEBERRY-ALMOND CLUSTERS
Replace the candied orange peel with 1 cup plus
1 tablespoon roughly chopped dried blueberries.

Chocolate-covered Almonds

IT'S HARD TO STOP EATING THESE ONCE YOU START.
I SOMETIMES SUBSTITUTE TOASTED AND SKINNED HAZELNUTS FOR THE ALMONDS.
I HAVE A HARD TIME DECIDING WHICH ONES I LIKE BETTER.

1¾ cups whole unblanched almonds
8 ounces bittersweet chocolate, finely chopped
⅓ cup unsweetened Dutch process cocoa powder
1 tablespoon plus 1 teaspoon confectioners' sugar

Center a rack in the oven and preheat to 350°F.

Spread the almonds on a jelly-roll pan and toast for 6 minutes. Stir well, then toast for another 6 minutes. Remove the pan from the oven and cool on a rack.

Melt the chocolate in the top of a double boiler over hot water, stirring often with a rubber spatula. Take the double boiler off the burner, take off the top pan, and place it over a larger bowl with about 1 inch of cool water. Stir the chocolate constantly to reduce its temperature to 90°F., about 10 minutes. Be careful not to allow any water to mix with the chocolate. To test if the chocolate is at the right temperature, use a chocolate or instant-read thermometer or place a dab below your lower lip. The chocolate should feel comfortable, not hot and not cold. When it reaches this temperature, remove the pan from the water and wipe the bottom and sides dry.

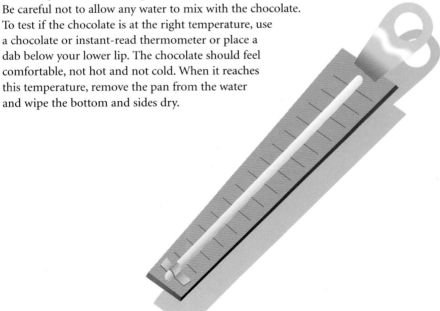

Place the almonds in a 2-quart mixing bowl and pour a third of the chocolate over them. Use a rubber spatula to mix and stir the almonds and chocolate together, completely coating the nuts. Continue to stir for a few minutes, until the chocolate begins to set up around the nuts. If the chocolate takes longer than about 6 minutes to set up, place the bowl in the refrigerator for 2 to 3 minutes, then separate any clusters that may have formed.

Pour half of the remaining chocolate over the nuts and stir again until the chocolate sets up around the nuts. Repeat with the remaining chocolate.

Sift the cocoa powder together with the confectioners' sugar or pulse them together in the workbowl of a food processor. Transfer the mixture to a large strong plastic bag. Place about half the almonds in the plastic bag, seal the top, and shake the bag well to coat the nuts.

Line a baking sheet with wax paper. Pour the nuts and cocoa mixture into a large strainer set over a bowl. Separate the nuts and place them on the baking sheet. Transfer the cocoa mixture to the plastic bag and repeat with the remaining almonds.

Serve the almonds at room temperature. Store them between layers of wax paper in an airtight container at room temperature for up to 2 weeks.

Makes about 3 cups nuts

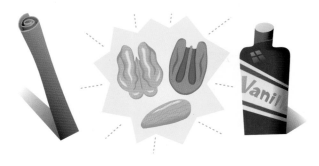

Cinnamon Nuts

CINNAMON ADDS A SPECIAL FLAVOR TO THESE SUGAR-GLAZED NUTS.
JUST ABOUT ANY NUT CAN BE USED FOR THIS RECIPE;
MY FAVORITES ARE WALNUTS AND ALMONDS.

2 teaspoons vegetable oil, such as canola, for the pan
1 cup sugar
½ teaspoon ground cinnamon
⅛ teaspoon cream of tartar
¼ cup hot water
½ teaspoon vanilla extract
1½ cups nuts

Coat a baking sheet or cake pan with the vegetable oil. Combine the sugar, cinnamon, cream of tartar, and water in a 2-quart heavy-bottomed saucepan. Cook the mixture over high heat until it reaches 246°F. on a candy thermometer, about 8 minutes. Using a damp pastry brush, wash down the sides of the pan 2 times while the mixture is cooking, to prevent sugar crystallization.

When the mixture is at the correct temperature, take the pan off of the heat and immediately stir in the vanilla. Stir in the nuts, using a long-handled wooden spoon. Continue to stir for another minute or two until the sugar syrup becomes cloudy. Turn the nuts out onto the baking sheet, using the wooden spoon to spread them out. Let the nuts cool briefly, about 5 minutes. Separate them with your fingers and let them cool completely.

Serve the nuts at room temperature. Store them between layers of wax paper in an airtight container at room temperature for up to 10 days.

Makes about 2½ cups nuts

Penuche Walnuts

PENUCHE (PRONOUNCED PEH-NOO-CHEE) COMES FROM THE MEXICAN WORD
FOR BROWN SUGAR AND USUALLY MEANS A FUDGELIKE CANDY MADE WITH
BROWN SUGAR, CREAM, AND NUTS. IN THIS RECIPE THE COMBINATION
OF BROWN SUGAR AND SOUR CREAM USED TO COAT THE WALNUTS
CREATES THE SAME DEEP FLAVOR. THESE TASTE SO GOOD THAT
THEY SEEM TO DISAPPEAR AS SOON AS THEY ARE SERVED.
TRY THIS WITH PECANS.

½ cup (firmly packed) golden brown sugar
¼ cup granulated sugar
¼ cup sour cream
½ teaspoon vanilla extract
1¼ cups walnut halves

Line a baking sheet with aluminum foil. Combine the brown sugar, granulated sugar, and sour cream in a 2-quart heavy-bottomed saucepan. Cook the mixture over medium heat, stirring frequently with a long-handled wooden spoon, until it registers 246°F. on a candy thermometer, about 12 minutes. Take the pan off of the heat and immediately blend in the vanilla. Stir in the walnuts and coat them completely with the mixture.

Turn the nuts out onto the baking sheet and let cool for 5 minutes. Separate them into individual nuts and let cool completely.

Serve the walnuts at room temperature. Store them between layers of wax paper in an airtight container at room temperature for up to 2 weeks.

Makes 2 cups nuts

Orange Candied Pecans

ORANGE ZEST AND FRESHLY SQUEEZED ORANGE JUICE GIVE
AN EXTRA-SPECIAL ZING TO THESE SUGAR-GLAZED NUTS.
OTHER NUTS CAN BE USED IN PLACE OF THE PECANS.

2 teaspoons vegetable oil, such as canola, for the pan
1 cup sugar
⅛ teaspoon cream of tartar
Zest of 1 medium orange, finely minced
¼ cup freshly squeezed orange juice
½ teaspoon vanilla extract
1½ cups pecan halves

Coat a baking sheet or cake pan with the vegetable oil.

Combine the sugar, cream of tartar, orange zest, and orange juice in a 2-quart heavy-bottomed saucepan. Cook the mixture over high heat until it reaches 246°F. on a candy thermometer, about 8 minutes. Using a damp pastry brush, wash down the sides of the pan 2 times while the mixture is cooking, to prevent sugar crystallization.

When the mixture is at the correct temperature, take the pan off of the heat and immediately stir in the vanilla. Stir in the nuts, using a long-handled wooden spoon. Continue to stir for another minute or two until the sugar syrup becomes shiny and tacky. Turn the nuts out onto the baking sheet, using the wooden spoon to spread them out. Let the nuts cool briefly, about 5 minutes. Separate them and leave to cool completely.

Serve the nuts at room temperature. Store them between layers of wax paper in an airtight container at room temperature for up to 10 days.

Makes about 2½ cups nuts

Chocolate Hazelnut Pyramids

TOASTED AND SKINNED HAZELNUTS AND DARK CHOCOLATE ARE THE
ONLY INGREDIENTS IN THIS SIMPLE CANDY. MILK CHOCOLATE OR
WHITE CHOCOLATE CAN BE SUBSTITUTED FOR THE DARK CHOCOLATE.

1½ cups hazelnuts
8 ounces bittersweet chocolate, finely chopped, for tempering (page 96)

Center a rack in the oven and preheat to 350°F.

Spread the hazelnuts on a jelly-roll pan or in a cake pan. Toast them until the skins blister and the nuts are light golden colored, 15 to 18 minutes. Remove the pan from the oven and cool on a rack for 10 minutes. Rub the hazelnuts between your hands or in a kitchen towel to remove most of the skins.

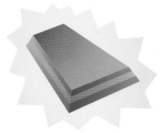

Line a baking sheet with parchment or wax paper. Melt and temper the chocolate, then hold the chocolate at the correct temperature by placing it over a pan of warm water. Stir the hazelnuts into the chocolate, coating them completely. Using a spoon, lift out 3 or 4 hazelnuts. Let the nuts gently drop from the spoon onto the baking sheet to form a pyramid. If using 3 nuts, make a base of two and place the third on top; if using 4 nuts, make a base of three and balance the fourth on top. When all the pyramids are formed, refrigerate for 15 minutes, to set the chocolate.

Place each pyramid in a paper candy cup and serve at room temperature. Store the pyramids between layers of wax paper in an airtight container wrapped with aluminum foil in the refrigerator for up to 3 weeks or in the freezer for up to 2 months.

Makes 36 to 48 pyramids

Pistachio-Almond Nougat

NOUGAT IS A CHEWY CONFECTION COMPOSED OF A MIXTURE OF STIFFLY BEATEN
EGG WHITES AND HOT SUGAR SYRUP BEATEN TOGETHER UNTIL COOL, THEN
MIXED WITH NUTS. NOUGAT IS SENSITIVE TO HUMIDITY AND WILL BECOME STICKY
IF EXPOSED TO TOO MUCH. ALTHOUGH THE COMBINATION OF PISTACHIO NUTS
AND ALMONDS IN THIS RECIPE IS SUPERB, OTHER NUTS CAN BE SUBSTITUTED.
DIPPING THE NOUGAT IN CHOCOLATE ADDS AN EXTRA-SPECIAL TOUCH.

¼ to ⅓ cup confectioners' sugar
⅔ cup honey
¾ cup sugar
½ vanilla bean, split lengthwise
1 large egg white, at room temperature
¼ teaspoon cream of tartar
2 cups slivered or whole blanched almonds
½ cup toasted unsalted pistachio nuts
12 ounces bittersweet or semisweet chocolate, finely chopped, for tempering (page 96)

Dust the back of a baking sheet heavily with confectioners' sugar. Place a 2-cup glass measure near the stove.

Combine the honey, sugar, and vanilla bean in a 2-quart heavy-bottomed saucepan. Cook the mixture over medium heat, stirring with a wooden spoon until liquid. Increase the heat to high and cook the syrup until it reaches 248° to 250°F. on a candy thermometer. Using a damp pastry brush, wash down the sides of the pan 2 times while the mixture is cooking, to prevent sugar crystallization.

At the same time, beat the egg white in the bowl of a stand mixer using the wire whip or in a mixing bowl using a hand-held mixer until it is foamy. Add the cream of tartar and continue beating until the egg white holds stiff peaks.

When the honey mixture is at the correct temperature, take the pan off of the heat and pour the syrup into the measuring cup, to stop the cooking. Use a fork to remove the vanilla bean. With the mixer on low speed pour the sugar syrup into the beaten egg white in a slow, steady stream. Then increase the mixer speed to medium and beat until the bottom of the bowl is cool to the touch, 12 to 15 minutes. Add the nuts and blend them in thoroughly.

Scrape the nougat from the bowl onto the prepared baking sheet. Dust the top of the nougat heavily with confectioners' sugar and use a heavy rolling pin to roll it into a rectangle about ⅜-inch thick. Be sure to keep the edges square and even. Cover the nougat loosely with wax paper and let it stand at room temperature for at least 6 hours to firm up.

Using a sharp serrated knife, cut the nougat into ¾ x 1½-inch rectangles. If the nougat is very sticky, refrigerate it for about 30 minutes.

Line 2 baking sheets with wax paper. Melt and temper the chocolate. Using a fork or dipping tool, dip the nougat in the chocolate, shaking off the excess as the pieces are lifted out. Place the pieces on the baking sheets. When all the pieces are dipped, refrigerate the candies for 15 minutes, to set the chocolate.

Place the nougat in paper candy cups and serve at room temperature. Store the nougat between layers of wax paper in an airtight container at room temperature for up to 1 week or in the refrigerator for up to 1 month.

Makes 60 pieces

Chocolate Walnut Roll

This recipe calls for a small amount of raw egg white.
There is ongoing concern about salmonella bacteria in raw eggs.
To avoid any problems with this be sure to buy your eggs from a reliable
source, make sure they are USDA inspected, keep them refrigerated,
and use them by the pull date on the carton.
It is not advisable for pregnant women to eat raw eggs.

1½ cups walnuts
4 ounces bittersweet or semisweet chocolate, very finely chopped or shaved
¼ to ⅓ cup confectioners' sugar
2½ teaspoons dark rum
2 teaspoons finely minced orange zest
1 tablespoon (about ½) egg white

Place the walnuts in the workbowl of a food processor
fitted with a steel blade. Pulse until the walnuts are finely
ground, about 1 minute. Remove ½ cup and set aside.
Add the finely chopped chocolate to the remaining
walnuts in the workbowl and pulse again for
20 seconds to combine.

Transfer the mixture to a 2-quart mixing
bowl. Add ¼ cup confectioners' sugar, the rum,
and orange zest, and toss the mixture to combine
the ingredients. Blend in the egg white and stir
the mixture until it is moist enough to be pressed
together and hold its shape. If the mixture is too
wet, add more confectioners' sugar as needed.
Cover the bowl with plastic wrap and
refrigerate for 30 minutes.

Divide the mixture in two. Using a piece of wax paper, shape each half into a 6 x 1-inch roll. Dredge the rolls in the remaining ½ cup of walnuts. Wrap each roll in wax paper, cover with plastic wrap, and refrigerate for 24 hours.

Just before serving, slice each roll into ½-inch-thick rounds and place them in paper candy cups. Store the chocolate walnut rolls tightly covered with plastic wrap and aluminum foil in the refrigerator for up to 3 weeks or in the freezer for up to 2 months.

Makes 24 rolls

Spiced Pecans

CINNAMON, CLOVES, NUTMEG, AND GINGER ADD THEIR
WARM, ROBUST FLAVORS TO THESE CRUNCHY NUTS.
BE SURE TO KEEP THEM IN AN AIRTIGHT CONTAINER,
SINCE THE LEAST BIT OF EXPOSURE TO HUMIDITY
CAN MAKE THEM SOGGY. WALNUTS CAN BE USED
IN PLACE OF THE PECANS.

¾ cup sugar
1½ teaspoons ground cinnamon
½ teaspoon ground cloves
½ teaspoon freshly grated nutmeg
½ teaspoon ground ginger
1 large egg white, at room temperature
1 tablespoon water
2 cups pecan halves

Center a rack in the oven and preheat to 275°F.

Combine the sugar and spices in a small mixing bowl and blend well. Beat the egg white with the water in a mixing bowl until it holds soft peaks. Gently fold the pecans into the egg white, coating them completely. Add the spice mixture and stir to coat the nuts thoroughly.

Turn the nuts out onto a jelly-roll pan, separating them as much as possible. Toast for 30 minutes. Remove the pan from the oven and loosen the nuts from the pan. Transfer the pecans to another baking sheet or jelly-roll pan, separate them as much as possible, and cool on a rack.

Serve the pecans at room temperature. Store them between layers of wax paper in an airtight container at room temperature for up to 3 weeks.

Makes 3 cups nuts

dynamite chocolate delights

Ganache Butter Cups

GANACHE IS A MIXTURE OF CHOCOLATE AND CREAM WITH A SILKY-SMOOTH
CONSISTENCY. FOR THIS CANDY, SOFTENED BUTTER IS BEATEN UNTIL FLUFFY AND
ADDED TO THE GANACHE, THEN THE MIXTURE IS PIPED INTO FOIL CANDY CUPS.

6 ounces bittersweet or semisweet chocolate, finely chopped
½ cup whipping cream
½ teaspoon vanilla extract
6 tablespoons unsalted butter, softened

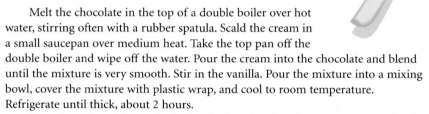

Melt the chocolate in the top of a double boiler over hot
water, stirring often with a rubber spatula. Scald the cream in
a small saucepan over medium heat. Take the top pan off the
double boiler and wipe off the water. Pour the cream into the chocolate and blend
until the mixture is very smooth. Stir in the vanilla. Pour the mixture into a mixing
bowl, cover the mixture with plastic wrap, and cool to room temperature.
Refrigerate until thick, about 2 hours.

Place the softened butter in the bowl of an electric mixer or in a mixing bowl.
Using the flat beater attachment or a hand-held mixer, beat the softened butter until it
is light and fluffy, about 3 minutes. Add the ganache to the butter, a few tablespoons
at a time, beating gently to mix well. When all of the ganache is added, the mixture
should be smooth and evenly blended.

Fit a 12-inch pastry bag with a large closed star tip (number 4) and fill the bag
partway with the ganache mixture. Pipe the ganache into 1-inch foil candy cups up
to the edge, making a swirl design on top. Chill the cups for about 1 hour.

Let ganache cups stand at room temperature for 20 minutes before serving to
develop their full flavor. Store the ganache cups in a single layer covered with wax
paper in an airtight container wrapped with aluminum foil in the refrigerator for
up to 3 weeks or in the freezer for up to 2 months.

Makes 36 cups

Variation:

GANACHE NUT CUPS

Stir ½ cup finely chopped toasted nuts, such as hazelnuts, into the ganache after adding
the vanilla. Use a large plain round tip (number 5 or 6) to pipe the mixture into the foil
cups. Top each ganache cup with a whole toasted nut.

Gianduia Swirls

GIANDUIA (PRONOUNCED JOHN-DOO-YA) IS A BLEND OF HAZELNUTS AND CHOCOLATE
WITH A UNIQUE FLAVOR AND A VELVETY SMOOTH TEXTURE. GIANDUIA REFERS TO A
TYPE OF CHOCOLATE USED AS AN INGREDIENT AND TO CONFECTIONS THAT CONTAIN
HAZELNUTS AND CHOCOLATE. FOR THESE CANDIES, NUTELLA, AN ITALIAN HAZELNUT-
CHOCOLATE SPREAD AVAILABLE IN SPECIALTY FOOD SHOPS AND GOURMET MARKETS,
IS BLENDED WITH BITTERSWEET CHOCOLATE. THE MIXTURE IS PIPED INTO
FOIL CANDY CUPS AND TOPPED WITH A WHOLE TOASTED AND SKINNED HAZELNUT.

4 ounces bittersweet or semisweet chocolate, finely chopped
½ cup Nutella, at room temperature
30 whole toasted and skinned hazelnuts

Melt the chocolate in the top of a double boiler over hot water, stirring often with
a rubber spatula. Take the top pan off of the double boiler and wipe off the water. Stir
in the Nutella until the mixture is thoroughly blended. Pour the mixture into a bowl,
cover with plastic wrap, and cool to room temperature. Refrigerate until the mixture
is the consistency of thick pudding, 45 minutes to 1 hour.

Fit a 12-inch pastry bag with a large open star tip (number 3) and fill the bag
partway with the gianduia mixture. Pipe it into 1-inch foil candy cups up to the edge,
making a swirl design on top. Place a whole toasted and
skinned hazelnut, pointed end up, in the center of each
gianduia cup. Chill the swirls for about 20 minutes.

Serve at room temperature. Store
the swirls in a single layer covered with
wax paper in an airtight container
wrapped with aluminum foil in the
refrigerator for up to 3 weeks or
in the freezer for up to 2 months.

Makes 30 swirls

Golden Mocha Palets

RICH COFFEE-FLAVORED CHOCOLATE GANACHE IS SHAPED INTO SMALL ROUND COINS,
DIPPED IN CHOCOLATE, AND DECORATED WITH GLISTENING FLECKS
OF EDIBLE GOLD LEAF. PURE 22- TO 24-KARAT GOLD LEAF IS AVAILABLE
IN 3½-INCH-SQUARE BOOKS OF 25 LEAVES AT ART SUPPLY STORES AND
SIGN PAINTERS' SUPPLY SHOPS. BE SURE TO USE PURE GOLD, NOT ALLOY.
IT IS BEST TO USE LOOSE LEAF, WHICH IS EXTREMELY THIN AND
EASIER TO HANDLE THAN PATENT LEAF, WHICH IS THICK AND
MUST BE CUT WITH A KNIFE OR SCISSORS.

10 ounces bittersweet or semisweet chocolate, finely chopped
⅔ cup whipping cream
1 tablespoon plus 1 teaspoon instant espresso powder
1 sheet 22- to 24-karat loose gold leaf
12 ounces bittersweet chocolate, finely chopped, for tempering (page 96)

Using wax paper, line an 8-inch square baking pan, extending the paper over the sides. Melt the 10 ounces of chocolate in the top of a double boiler over hot water, stirring often with a rubber spatula. Scald the cream in a small saucepan over medium heat. Add the espresso powder and stir it to dissolve. Take the top pan off of the double boiler and wipe off the water. Pour the cream into the chocolate and stir together with a rubber spatula until the mixture is smooth. Pour the mixture into the prepared pan, cover the top loosely with wax paper, then tightly with plastic wrap. Cool to room temperature, then refrigerate until firm, about 3 hours.

Line a baking sheet with wax paper. Remove the pan from the refrigerator. Holding the ends of the wax paper, lift the mixture from the pan and place it on a smooth, flat work surface. Using a 1-inch-diameter plain round cutter dipped in hot water and dried, cut the mixture into circles. Using a small offset spatula, also dipped in hot water and dried, transfer the chocolate coins or palets to the baking sheet. Cover loosely with wax paper, then tightly with plastic wrap. Chill in the freezer for 2 hours.

Line another baking sheet with wax paper. Using a ⅛-inch-wide sable-hair art brush, gently lift the sheet of gold leaf and carefully transfer it to the baking sheet. Using the brush, crumble it into small pieces and scatter them over the wax paper. Be careful not to move too fast; the gold is very light and will fly into the air with too much movement.

Melt and temper the 12 ounces of chocolate. Remove the baking sheet from the freezer. Using a fork or a round chocolate dipping tool, dip a palet in the chocolate and shake off the excess as it is lifted out. Turn the palet upside down onto the gold leaf, letting it gently slide off the fork or dipper. When all the palets are dipped, refrigerate them on the baking sheet for 15 minutes, to set the chocolate.

Place each palet, gold side up, in a paper candy cup and serve at room temperature. Store the palets between layers of wax paper in an airtight container wrapped with aluminum foil in the refrigerator for up to 3 weeks or in the freezer for up to 2 months.

Makes 48 palets

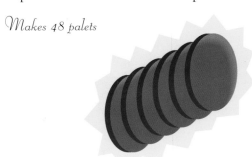

Chocolate Ingots

THE IDEA FOR THIS CANDY CAME DURING A TRIP TO PARIS,
WHERE I HUNTED FOR THE BEST CHOCOLATE CANDIES AND CONFECTIONS IN TOWN.
AFTER TASTING A RECTANGULAR HAZELNUT-FILLED CHOCOLATE BAR
AT ONE OF THE TOP *CHOCOLATIERS*, I CREATED THIS CANDY,
WHICH I THINK RANKS RIGHT UP THERE
WITH THE PARISIAN VERSION.

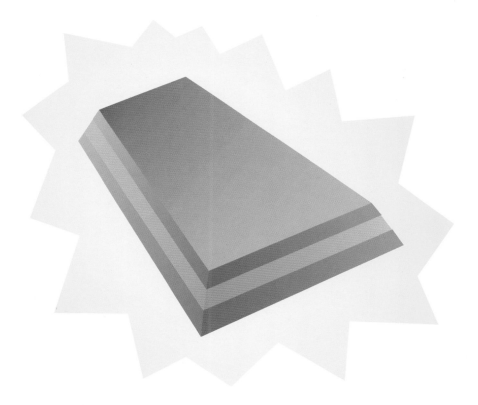

½ cup hazelnuts
2 tablespoons vegetable oil, such as canola
12 ounces bittersweet chocolate, finely chopped, for tempering (page 96)

Center a rack in the oven and preheat to 350°F.

Place the hazelnuts on a jelly-roll pan and toast them for 15 minutes. The skins will split and the nuts will turn golden brown. Remove the pan from the oven and cool on a rack for 10 to 15 minutes. Rub the hazelnuts between your hands or in a kitchen towel to remove most of the skins.

Place the hazelnuts and the vegetable oil in the workbowl of a food processor fitted with a steel blade. Pulse together until the mixture reaches a smooth and creamy consistency, about 1 minute. Transfer the hazelnut paste to a bowl and set aside.

Melt and temper the chocolate. Using a spoon, fill six 2 x 4-inch rectangular metal molds up to the top edge. Let the chocolate stand in the molds for 1 minute. Turn the molds upside down over the bowl of chocolate and let the chocolate drip out of the molds. This will leave a thin coating of chocolate in the mold.

Place a large spoonful of hazelnut paste in a line in the center of each chocolate-lined mold. Be careful not to let the hazelnut paste come up to the top of the mold. Use a spoon to fill each mold with the remaining chocolate, just up to the top edge. When each mold is filled, tap it gently a few times against the countertop. This helps the chocolate to spread evenly in the mold and to release any air bubbles that would form holes in the chocolate when it is set. Transfer the molds to a baking sheet and place it on a flat surface in the freezer. Leave the molds in the freezer to set for at least 30 minutes.

Take the molds out of the freezer and gently tap each mold several times against a countertop. Slip the ingot from the mold. Turn the unmolded ingots upside down, so the bottom becomes the top.

Serve the ingots at room temperature. Store the ingots between layers of wax paper in an airtight container wrapped with aluminum foil in the refrigerator for up to 3 weeks or in the freezer for up to 2 months.

Makes 6 ingots

Miniature Chocolate-Lemon Bars

THIS CANDY WAS INSPIRED BY ONE I TASTED IN A WORLD-FAMOUS
PARISIAN CHOCOLATE SHOP. FRESHLY GRATED LEMON ZEST ADDS A SPIRITED
BURST OF FLAVOR TO THE CREAMY DARK CHOCOLATE CENTER
OF THESE CHOCOLATE-COVERED CANDIES.

8 ounces bittersweet chocolate, finely chopped
½ cup whipping cream
2 large lemons
12 ounces bittersweet chocolate, finely chopped, for tempering (page 96)

Line a baking sheet with wax paper. Place an 8 x 4½-inch open metal flan form
in the center of the pan. Or line a 9 x 5-inch loaf pan with wax paper, letting it extend
over the sides.

Melt the 8 ounces of chocolate in the top of a double boiler over hot water, stirring
often with a rubber spatula. Scald the cream in a small saucepan over medium heat.
Take the top pan off the double boiler and wipe off the water. Pour the cream into the
chocolate and blend with a rubber spatula until the mixture is smooth. Finely grate
the zest of the lemons into the ganache. (Be careful not to grate any of the bitter white
pith under the zest.) Stir to blend well. Pour the mixture into the flan form or loaf pan,
cover the top loosely with wax paper, then tightly with plastic wrap. Refrigerate until
firm, about 3 hours.

Remove the pan from the refrigerator. Using a sharp thin-bladed knife dipped in
hot water and dried, loosen the mixture from the flan form. If using the loaf pan, lift
the edges of the wax paper to remove the mixture from the pan. Gently peel off the
wax paper.

Line a baking sheet with wax paper. Dip the knife in hot water and dry it and cut the chocolate into ½-inch-wide slices. Cut each slice in half to form bars. Transfer the bars to the baking sheet, cover loosely with wax paper, then tightly with plastic wrap. Chill in the freezer for at least 2 hours.

Line another baking sheet with wax paper. Melt and temper the chocolate. Remove the pan of bars from the freezer. Using a fork or dipping tool, dip a bar in the chocolate, shaking off the excess as it is lifted out. Let the bar gently slide off the fork onto the baking sheet. Touch the top with the tines of the fork to make a design. When all the bars are dipped, refrigerate the baking sheet for 15 minutes, to set the chocolate.

Place each bar in a paper candy cup and serve at room temperature. Store the bars between layers of wax paper in an airtight container wrapped with aluminum foil in the refrigerator for up to 3 weeks or in the freezer for up to 2 months.

Makes 32 bars

Coconut Haystacks

THIS IS ONE OF THE EASIEST CANDIES TO MAKE—AND TO EAT.
VARIATIONS CAN BE CREATED BY REPLACING PART OF THE TOASTED COCONUT
WITH RAISINS OR BY SUBSTITUTING A MIXTURE OF RAISINS AND
SALTED TOASTED PEANUTS FOR THE COCONUT.

1¾ cups shredded or flaked sweetened coconut
7 ounces bittersweet or semisweet chocolate, finely chopped

Center a rack in the oven and preheat to 325°F.

Place the coconut in a cake pan or pie plate and toast it for 4 or 5 minutes, stirring after every minute. Remove from the oven and cool completely on a rack.

Melt the chocolate in the top of a double boiler over hot water, stirring often with a rubber spatula. Take the double boiler off the heat, take off the top pan, and place it over a larger bowl with about an inch of cool water. Gently stir the chocolate to reduce the temperature to 95°F. about 8 minutes. Be careful not to allow any water to mix with the chocolate. To test if the chocolate is at the right temperature, use a chocolate or instant-read thermometer or place a dab below your lower lip. The chocolate should feel comfortable, not hot and not cold. When it reaches this temperature, replace the pan of chocolate over the pan of warm water.

Line a baking sheet with wax paper. Add the toasted coconut to the chocolate and stir to coat it completely. Using a spoon, form 1-inch-diameter mounds and place them on the baking sheet. Refrigerate for 15 minutes to set the chocolate.

Place each round in a paper candy cup and serve at room temperature. Store the haystacks between layers of wax paper in an airtight container wrapped with aluminum foil in the refrigerator for up to 3 weeks or in the freezer for up to 2 months.

Makes 30 haystacks

Molded Chocolate-Orange Candy Bars

FINELY CHOPPED CANDIED ORANGE PEEL IS UNITED WITH CHOCOLATE
FOR THIS CANDY BAR. NUMEROUS SHAPES AND SIZES OF BAR MOLDS
ARE AVAILABLE FOR MAKING THIS CANDY.

12 ounces bittersweet, semisweet, milk, or white chocolate, finely chopped,
    for tempering (page 96)
½ cup finely chopped candied orange peel (page 94)

Melt and temper the chocolate. Stir in the candied orange peel. Carefully pour the
mixture into the molds, filling them just to the top edge. Gently tap the filled molds
against a countertop a few times to release any air bubbles that would form holes in
the chocolate when it is set. Transfer the molds to a baking sheet and place it on a flat
surface in the freezer for 20 minutes.

Place a piece of wax paper on a smooth work surface or a baking sheet. Take the
chocolate molds out of the freezer. Turn a mold upside down over the wax paper and
holding it by opposite edges, gently bend it back and forth. The chocolate bars should
slip out of the mold easily. If they don't, place the mold back in the freezer for another
15 minutes.

Serve the bars at room temperature. Store the chocolate bars between layers of
wax paper in an airtight container at room temperature for 2 weeks or wrap the
container in aluminum foil and store it in the refrigerator for up to 1 month or
in the freezer for up to 2 months.

Makes two 3 x 6½-inch bars and four 2¼ x 3½-inch bars

marzipan madness

Walnut Marzipan Rounds

MARZIPAN IS A CONFECTION MADE OF VERY FINELY GROUND ALMONDS AND SUGAR.
IT HAS A PLIABLE TEXTURE SIMILAR TO PIE DOUGH. YOU CAN BUY READY-MADE
MARZIPAN IN 7-OUNCE PLASTIC-WRAPPED ROLLS IN THE IMPORTED FOOD SECTION
IN MOST LARGE SUPERMARKETS, IN GOURMET FOOD SHOPS, AND COOKWARE SHOPS.
FOR THESE ELEGANT CANDIES, THE MARZIPAN IS MIXED WITH FINELY GROUND
WALNUTS, SLICED INTO ROUNDS, DIPPED IN CHOCOLATE, AND
CROWNED WITH A WALNUT HALF.

3 to 4 tablespoons confectioners' sugar
1 roll (7 ounces) marzipan
⅓ cup finely ground walnuts
1 tablespoon Nocello or other nut-flavored liqueur, optional
6 ounces bittersweet, semisweet, or white chocolate, finely
    chopped, for tempering (page 96)
22 walnut halves

Line 2 baking sheets with wax paper. Sprinkle some of the confectioners' sugar
on a smooth work surface. Place the roll of marzipan on the work surface and make
several indentations in it with your fingers. Sprinkle the ground walnuts and liqueur,
if using, into the indentations and knead the mass together until it is smooth and well
blended. If necessary, use more confectioners' sugar to prevent the marzipan from
sticking. Roll the marzipan into a 10 x 1-inch log. Cut the log into ½-inch rounds,
place the rounds on one of the baking sheets, and let them air dry for 30 minutes.

Melt and temper the chocolate. Using a fork or dipping tool, dip each marzipan
round into the chocolate, shaking off the excess as it is lifted out. Place the round on
the other baking sheet and press a walnut half on top before the chocolate sets up.
When all the rounds are dipped, refrigerate them for 15 minutes, to set the chocolate.

Place each round in a paper candy cup and serve at room temperature. Store the
marzipan rounds between layers of wax paper in an airtight container wrapped with
aluminum foil in the refrigerator for up to 3 weeks or in the freezer for up to 2 months.

Makes 22 rounds

Variation:

WALNUT MARZIPAN HEARTS

After kneading the marzipan, roll it out with a rolling pin to a thickness of ⅛ inch. Using a 1-inch heart-shape cutter, cut the marzipan. Transfer the hearts to a lined baking sheet and let them air dry for 30 minutes. Melt and temper the chocolate. Using a fork or dipping tool, dip the hearts in the chocolate, shaking off the excess as they are lifted out. Place the hearts on a lined baking sheet and center a walnut half or quarter on top before the chocolate sets up. Or hold the hearts in your fingertips and dip them halfway into the chocolate, coating 1 side. Place them on a lined baking sheet. Either way, after all the hearts are dipped, refrigerate the pan for 15 minutes, to set the chocolate. Place each heart in a paper candy cup and serve at room temperature.

Pistachio Marzipan Balls

PISTACHIO NUTS AND MARZIPAN ARE BLENDED WITH A SPLASH OF AMARETTO,
SHAPED INTO BALLS, AND DIPPED IN WHITE CHOCOLATE TO
MAKE THESE MOCK-TRUFFLE CANDIES.
YOU CAN SUBSTITUTE MACADAMIA NUTS FOR THE PISTACHIOS.

⅓ cup confectioners' sugar, in a dredger
1 roll (7 ounces) marzipan
½ cup finely chopped toasted pistachio nuts
1 tablespoon amaretto or cognac
8 ounces white chocolate, finely chopped, for tempering (page 96)

Sprinkle some of the confectioners' sugar on a smooth work surface. Place the roll of marzipan on the work surface and make several indentations in it with your fingers. Set aside 2 teaspoons of the ground pistachio nuts and sprinkle the rest into the indentations in the marzipan. Add the amaretto and knead the mass together until it is smooth and well blended. If necessary, use more confectioners' sugar to prevent the marzipan from sticking.

Line 2 baking sheets with wax paper. Pinch off pieces of the marzipan mixture and roll into 1-inch balls. Place the balls on one of the baking sheets.

Melt and temper the white chocolate. Using a fork or dipping tool, dip a marzipan ball into the chocolate, shaking off the excess as it is lifted out. Turn the ball out onto the other baking sheet and sprinkle a pinch of ground pistachio nuts on top before the chocolate sets up. When all the balls are dipped, refrigerate them for 15 minutes, to set the chocolate.

Place each marzipan ball in a paper candy cup and serve at room temperature. Store the marzipan balls between layers of wax paper in an airtight container wrapped with aluminum foil in the refrigerator for up to 3 weeks or in the freezer for up to 2 months.

Makes 30 balls

Hazelnut Marzipan Balls

THESE DECEPTIVE LITTLE CANDIES LOOK LIKE TRUFFLES,
BUT WHEN YOU BITE INTO ONE, YOU GET AN EYE-OPENING SURPRISE.

⅓ cup confectioners' sugar, in a dredger
1 roll (7 ounces) marzipan
½ cup finely ground toasted and skinned hazelnuts
1 tablespoon Frangelico
8 ounces bittersweet or semisweet chocolate, finely chopped, for tempering (page 96)

Sprinkle some of the confectioners' sugar on a smooth work surface. Place the roll of marzipan on the work surface and make several indentations in it with your fingers. Set aside 2 teaspoons of the ground hazelnuts and sprinkle the rest into the indentations in the marzipan. Add the Frangelico and knead the mass together until it is smooth and well blended. If necessary, use more confectioners' sugar to prevent the marzipan from sticking.

Line 2 baking sheets with wax paper. Pinch off pieces of the marzipan mixture and roll into 1-inch balls. Place the balls on one of the baking sheets.

Melt and temper the chocolate. Using a fork or dipping tool, dip a marzipan ball into the chocolate, shaking off the excess as it is lifted out. Turn the ball out onto the other baking sheet and sprinkle a pinch of ground hazelnuts on top before the chocolate sets up. When all the balls are dipped, refrigerate them for 15 minutes, to set the chocolate.

Place each marzipan ball in a paper candy cup and serve at room temperature. Store the marzipan balls between layers of wax paper in an airtight container wrapped with aluminum foil in the refrigerator for up to 3 weeks or in the freezer for up to 2 months.

Makes 30 balls

Cherry Marzipan Wedges

DRIED CHERRIES AND CHERRY BRANDY GIVE MARZIPAN AN
UNEXPECTED FLAVOR TWIST. FOR AN ADDED HIGHLIGHT,
DIP ONE END OF THE WEDGE IN CHOCOLATE.

3 to 4 tablespoons confectioners' sugar, in a dredger
1 roll (7 ounces) marzipan
3 tablespoons finely chopped dried cherries plus 36 slivers dried cherry
1 tablespoon kirschwasser, optional
6 ounces bittersweet chocolate, finely chopped, for tempering (page 96), optional

Line a baking sheet with wax paper. Sprinkle some of the confectioners' sugar on a smooth work surface. Place the roll of marzipan on the work surface and make several indentations in it with your fingers. Sprinkle the dried cherries and kirschwasser, if using, into the indentations and knead the mass together until it is smooth and well blended. If necessary, use more confectioners' sugar to prevent the marzipan from sticking. With a rolling pin, roll out the marzipan ⅛ inch thick. Using a 2-inch-wide diamond-shape cutter, cut the marzipan. Cut each diamond in half across the width, to make 2 wedges. Place the wedges on the baking sheet, press a sliver of dried cherry into the center of each wedge, and let the wedges air dry for 30 minutes.

Line another baking sheet with wax paper. Melt and temper the chocolate, if using. Hold a marzipan wedge by one of the points and dip another point into the chocolate, shaking off the excess as it is lifted out. Place the wedge on the baking sheet. Refrigerate the candies for 15 minutes, to set the chocolate. Serve the wedges at room temperature. Store the marzipan wedges between layers of wax paper in an airtight container wrapped with aluminum foil in the refrigerator for up to 3 weeks or in the freezer for up to 2 months.

Makes 36 wedges

Orange Marzipan Squares

ORANGE, ORANGE, AND MORE ORANGE GOES INTO THESE TEMPTING
CHOCOLATE-DIPPED SQUARES.

½ cup confectioners' sugar, in a dredger
1 roll (7 ounces) marzipan
3 tablespoons finely chopped candied orange peel plus 36 slivers
    candied orange peel (page 94)
1 tablespoon Grand Marnier or other orange liqueur
8 ounces bittersweet or semisweet chocolate, finely chopped, for tempering (page 96)

Sprinkle some of the confectioners' sugar on a smooth work surface. Place the roll of marzipan on the work surface and make several indentations in it with your fingers. Sprinkle the chopped candied orange peel and the Grand Marnier into the indentations and knead the mass together until it is smooth and well blended. If necessary, use more confectioners' sugar to prevent the marzipan from sticking.

Sprinkle more of the confectioners' sugar on the work surface and roll out the marzipan to a 6-inch square that is ½-inch thick. With a sharp knife, cut the square into six 1-inch-wide rows, then cut each row into six 1-inch-wide pieces. Line 2 baking sheets with wax paper. Place the marzipan squares on one of the baking sheets. Cover with plastic wrap and refrigerate until firm, 1 hour.

Melt and temper the chocolate. Remove the marzipan squares from the refrigerator. Using a fork or dipping tool, dip a square in the tempered chocolate and coat it completely. Lift the square from the chocolate, carefully shaking off the excess. Place the square onto the other baking sheet and center a sliver of candied orange peel on top before the chocolate sets up. When all the squares are dipped, refrigerate for 15 minutes, to set the chocolate.

Place each marzipan square in a paper candy cup and serve at room temperature. Store the marzipan squares between layers of wax paper in an airtight container wrapped with aluminum foil in the refrigerator for up to 3 weeks or in the freezer for up to 2 months.

Makes 36 squares

Variation:

ALMOND MARZIPAN SQUARES
Replace the candied orange peel with ¼ cup finely chopped toasted slivered almonds and replace the Grand Marnier with amaretto.

Coconut Marzipan Coins

DARK CHOCOLATE MIXED WITH TOASTED COCONUT IS USED TO DIP THESE ORANGE-FLAVORED MARZIPAN ROUNDS.

1 cup shredded or flaked sweetened coconut
2 tablespoons Grand Marnier or other orange-flavored liqueur
3 to 4 tablespoons confectioners' sugar
1 roll (7 ounces) marzipan
6 ounces bittersweet or semisweet chocolate, finely chopped, for tempering (page 96)

Center a rack in the oven and preheat to 325°F.

Place the coconut in a cake pan or pie plate. Sprinkle 1 tablespoon of the Grand Marnier over the coconut and toss to blend well. Toast the coconut in the oven for 12 minutes, stirring every 3 minutes. Take the pan out of the oven and cool completely on a rack.

Sprinkle some of the confectioners' sugar on a smooth work surface. Place the roll of marzipan on the work surface and make several indentations in it. Sprinkle the Grand Marnier in the indentations and knead the mass together until it is smooth and well blended. If necessary, add more confectioners' sugar to prevent the marzipan from sticking.

Line 2 baking sheets with wax paper. Sprinkle the work surface again with some of the confectioners' sugar and roll the marzipan into a 16 x ¾-inch log. Cut into ½-inch-thick rounds, place the coins on one of the baking sheets, and let them air dry for 30 minutes.

Melt and temper the chocolate. Add the toasted coconut to the chocolate and stir to blend thoroughly. Using a fork or dipping tool, dip each marzipan coin into the chocolate, shaking off the excess as it is lifted out. Place the coins on the other baking sheet. Refrigerate the coins for 15 minutes, to set the chocolate.

Place each coin in a paper candy cup and serve at room temperature. Store the marzipan coins between layers of wax paper in an airtight container wrapped with aluminum foil in the refrigerator for up to 3 weeks or in the freezer for up to 2 months.

Makes 32 coins

beautiful brittles
and tempting toffees

Pine Nut Brittle

THIS IS A CLASSIC NUT BRITTLE WITH A NEW TWIST—PINE NUTS.
THEIR SPECIAL QUALITIES GIVE THIS CANDY A TASTE OF THE SOUTHWEST.

1 tablespoon plus ½ teaspoon unsalted butter, softened
1 cup sugar
½ cup water
¼ cup light corn syrup
Pinch of salt
1 cup pine nuts
½ teaspoon vanilla extract
½ teaspoon baking soda

Coat the back of a baking sheet and the blade of an offset spatula with 1 tablespoon of the butter.

Combine the sugar, water, and corn syrup in a 2-quart heavy-bottomed saucepan. Cook the mixture over high heat until it registers 310°F. on a candy thermometer, 12 to 15 minutes. Using a damp pastry brush, wash down the sides of the pan 2 times while the mixture is cooking, to prevent sugar crystallization. Using a long-handled wooden spoon, quickly stir in the salt and pine nuts, coating them completely.

Off the heat, combine the vanilla and baking soda in a small bowl. Add to the brittle mixture and stir until well blended. Quickly stir in the remaining ½ teaspoon of butter.

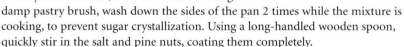

Turn the brittle out onto the baking sheet and work quickly to spread it out as thin as you can with the wooden spoon. Let cool for 5 minutes. Using the offset spatula, run it under the brittle to loosen it from the pan. Let cool completely.

Break the brittle into pieces and serve at room temperature. Store the brittle between layers of wax paper in an airtight container at room temperature for up to 1 week.

Makes 4¼ cups

Hazelnut-Almond Brittle

THIS TWO-NUT BRITTLE IS MADE WITH THE TECHNIQUE
OF DRY COOKING SUGAR. IN ORDER TO KEEP IT FROM BECOMING LUMPY,
THE SUGAR MUST BE STIRRED CONSTANTLY. OTHER NUTS CAN BE SUBSTITUTED
FOR THE HAZELNUTS AND ALMONDS.

⅓ cup hazelnuts
⅓ cup sliced almonds
3 tablespoons vegetable oil, such as canola
1 cup superfine or granulated sugar
¼ teaspoon freshly squeezed lemon juice

Center a rack in the oven and preheat to 350°F.

Place the hazelnuts in a cake pan or jelly-roll pan and toast for 15 minutes.
Remove the pan from the oven and cool on a rack for 10 minutes. Rub the hazelnuts
between your hands or in a kitchen towel to remove most of the skins. Finely chop
the hazelnuts and transfer them to a 2-cup mixing bowl. Place the almonds in a cake
pan or pie plate and toast for 6 minutes, shaking the pan after 3 minutes. Remove the
pan from the oven and cool on a rack. Finely chop the almonds and mix them with
the hazelnuts.

Oil the back of a baking sheet, a metal or marble rolling pin, and the cutter of a
pizza wheel with the vegetable oil. Heat ¼ cup of the sugar in a heavy saucepan over
medium-high heat, stirring constantly with a long-handled wooden spoon. The sugar
will start to melt. When it is completely liquid, slowly add another tablespoon of the
sugar and stir constantly until it is also melted. Continue adding the sugar a tablespoon
at a time, stirring constantly, until it is all liquid.

Take the pan off the heat and quickly blend in the lemon juice. Add the chopped
nuts and stir to cover them thoroughly with the caramel. Quickly turn the mixture out
onto the oiled pan and roll it out very thin. Using the oiled pizza wheel, cut the brittle
into 1-inch squares before it sets up. Leave the brittle to cool completely at room
temperature, about 30 minutes.

Break the brittle where scored and serve at room temperature. Store the brittle
between layers of wax paper in an airtight container at room temperature for
up to 3 weeks.

Makes 36 pieces

Classic Butterscotch

BUTTERSCOTCH IS A HARD CANDY THAT WAS CREATED IN EIGHTEENTH-CENTURY SCOTLAND. A COMBINATION OF SUGAR, CORN SYRUP, AND BUTTER IS COOKED TO A HIGH TEMPERATURE, RESULTING IN A DEEP, DISTINCTIVE FLAVOR. THIS RECIPE IS GOOD OLD-FASHIONED BUTTERSCOTCH AT ITS FINEST.

1 tablespoon unsalted butter, softened, for the pan and knife
2 cups (firmly packed) golden brown sugar
½ cup light corn syrup
8 tablespoons (1 stick) unsalted butter, cut into small pieces
1 tablespoon distilled white vinegar
½ cup water
2 teaspoons vanilla extract

Using aluminum foil, line an 8-inch square baking pan, extending the foil over the sides. Use the tablespoon of butter to butter the foil and the blade of a small chef's knife.

Combine the brown sugar, corn syrup, the 8 tablespoons of butter, vinegar, and water in a 3-quart heavy-bottomed saucepan over medium heat, stirring constantly with a long-handled wooden spoon until the sugar is dissolved, about 3 minutes. Using a damp pastry brush, wash down the sides of the pan 2 times while the mixture is cooking, to prevent sugar crystallization.

Raise the heat to high, place a candy thermometer in the pan, and cook the mixture, undisturbed, until it registers 290°F. on the thermometer, about 25 minutes.

Remove the pan from the heat, quickly stir in the vanilla, and pour the mixture into the prepared pan. Let stand for 10 minutes. Using the buttered knife, score the candy into 8 rows across each side. Let cool completely on a rack. Lift the butterscotch from the pan by the foil, turn it out onto a cutting board, remove the foil from the back, and turn the butterscotch right side up. Using a large chef's knife, cut the butterscotch where scored.

Serve the butterscotch at room temperature. Store the butterscotch between layers of wax paper in an airtight container at room temperature for up to 10 days.

Makes 64 pieces

Traditional Toffee

IF YOU ALLOW IT TO LINGER, THIS INCREDIBLE TOFFEE WILL MELT IN YOUR MOUTH.
IT'S BETTER THAN THE WELL-KNOWN TOFFEE MADE IN ENGLAND.

1 tablespoon unsalted butter, softened, for the pan and knife
1¾ cups granulated sugar
½ cup whipping cream
¼ teaspoon cream of tartar
Pinch of salt
12 tablespoons (1½ sticks) unsalted butter, cut into small pieces
1 teaspoon vanilla extract

Using aluminum foil, line an 8-inch-square baking pan, extending the foil over the sides. Use the tablespoon of butter to butter the foil and the blade of a small chef's knife.

Combine the sugar, cream, cream of tartar, and salt in a 3-quart heavy-bottomed saucepan. Cook over medium heat, stirring constantly with a long-handled wooden spoon to dissolve the sugar, about 3 minutes. Using a damp pastry brush, wash down the sides of the pan 2 times to prevent sugar crystallization. Add the 12 tablespoons of butter and stir often until it melts, about 5 minutes.

Raise the heat to high, place a candy thermometer in the pan, and cook the mixture, stirring often, until it reaches 290°F. on the thermometer, about 15 minutes.

Take the pan off the heat, quickly stir in the vanilla, and pour the mixture into the pan. Let stand for 5 minutes to cool. Using the buttered knife, score it into 8 rows each way. Let the toffee cool completely on a rack. Lift the toffee from the pan by the foil, turn it out onto a cutting board, remove the foil from the back, and turn the toffee right side up. Using a large chef's knife, cut the toffee where scored.

Serve the toffee at room temperature. Store the toffee between layers of wax paper in an airtight container at room temperature for up to 10 days.

Makes 64 pieces

Almond Buttercrunch Toffee Fingers

BUTTER, ALMONDS, SUGAR, AND CORN SYRUP JOIN FORCES
IN A HARD-TO-RESIST TREAT.

2 tablespoons unsalted butter, softened, for the baking sheet
8 tablespoons (1 stick) unsalted butter, cut into small pieces
½ cup sugar
1 tablespoon light corn syrup
Pinch of salt
1 cup toasted sliced almonds, roughly chopped

Coat the back of a baking sheet and the wheel of a pizza cutter with the
2 tablespoons of butter.

Combine the 8 tablespoons of butter, the sugar, corn syrup, and salt in a 2-quart
heavy-bottomed saucepan. Cook over medium-high heat, stirring with a long-handled
wooden spoon, until the mixture is liquid, about 4 minutes. Raise the heat to high, add
the almonds, and cook, stirring constantly, until the mixture is a light caramel color,
6 to 7 minutes.

Immediately turn the mixture out onto the baking sheet and spread it out into
a large rectangle with the wooden spoon. Using the pizza wheel, cut the
toffee into thin 2 x ¾-inch fingers. Let the toffee cool completely, about
30 minutes, then separate the cut pieces.

Serve the toffee at room temperature. Store the toffee
between layers of wax paper in an airtight container at
room temperature for up to 10 days.

Makes 60 fingers

Variation:

ALMOND BUTTERCRUNCH TOFFEE SQUARES Double the ingredients,
except for the butter used for the pan. Line an 8-inch-square baking pan with foil,
extending it over the sides, and butter the foil. After cooking the toffee, pour it into
the pan, and let it cool for 5 minutes. Using a buttered knife, score it into 8 rows in each
direction making 1-inch squares. To make a good thing even better, dip the toffee
squares into tempered bittersweet, semisweet, or milk chocolate.

Makes 64 squares

Toasted Pecan Toffee

BROWN SUGAR AND TOASTED PECANS GIVE THIS TOFFEE ITS ROBUST FLAVOR.
IT TASTES EVEN BETTER A DAY OR TWO AFTER IT'S MADE.

1½ cups pecans
1 tablespoon unsalted butter, softened, for the baking sheet and offset spatula
½ cup granulated sugar
3 tablespoons golden brown sugar
9 tablespoons (1 stick plus 1 tablespoon) unsalted butter, cut into small pieces
4½ tablespoons water
Pinch of salt

Center a rack in the oven and preheat to 350°F.

Spread the pecans in a cake pan or jelly-roll pan and toast for 3 minutes. Shake the pan and toast for another 3 minutes. Cool the pan on a rack and coarsely chop the pecans.

Coat the back of a baking sheet and the blade of an offset spatula with the tablespoon of butter. Combine the granulated sugar, brown sugar, the 9 tablespoons of butter, water, and salt in a 2-quart heavy-bottomed saucepan. Cook the mixture over medium heat, stirring occasionally with a long-handled wooden spoon, to melt the butter, about 5 minutes.

Raise the heat to high, place a candy thermometer in the pan, and cook the mixture, stirring constantly, until it reaches 310°F. on a candy thermometer, about 10 minutes. Quickly stir in the pecans. Immediately turn the toffee out onto the baking sheet and work quickly to spread it out to a large rectangle with the wooden spoon.

Let cool for 5 minutes. Using the offset spatula, run it under the toffee to loosen it from the pan. Let cool completely. Break the toffee into pieces.

Serve the toffee at room temperature. Store the toffee between pieces of wax paper in an airtight container at room temperature for up to 1 week.

Makes 4 cups

Hazelnut Chocolate Toffee

THIS CANDY COMBINES THREE OF MY FAVORITES—
BUTTERY TOFFEE, BITTERSWEET CHOCOLATE, AND TOASTED HAZELNUTS.
I LOOK FOR ANY EXCUSE TO MAKE THIS.

1 cup hazelnuts
1½ cups sugar
½ tablespoon unsalted butter, softened, for the dish
8 tablespoons (1 stick) unsalted butter, cut into small pieces
2 tablespoons plus 2 teaspoons water
1 teaspoon vanilla extract
3 ounces bittersweet chocolate, finely chopped or shaved

Center a rack in the oven and preheat to 350°F.

Place the hazelnuts on a jelly-roll pan and toast them until the skins split and the nuts turn an even golden brown color, about 15 minutes. Remove the pan from the oven and cool on a rack for 10 to 15 minutes. Rub the hazelnuts between your hands or in a kitchen towel to remove most of the skins.

Place the hazelnuts and 1½ tablespoons of the sugar in the workbowl of a food processor fitted with a steel blade. Pulse them together until the nuts are very finely ground, about 1 minute.

Coat the inside of an 11 x 7-inch glass baking dish heavily with the half tablespoon of butter and sprinkle half of the ground hazelnuts over the bottom of the pan in an even layer.

Combine the remaining sugar, the 8 tablespoons of butter, and water in a 2-quart heavy-bottomed saucepan and cook over medium heat, stirring often to melt the butter. Raise the heat to high and cook, stirring constantly with a long-handled wooden spoon, until the mixture reaches 280°F. on a candy thermometer, about 8 minutes. Remove the pan from the heat and quickly stir in the vanilla.

Immediately turn the mixture out into the baking dish and spread it over the bottom with the wooden spoon. Sprinkle the chocolate evenly over the warm toffee; it will melt immediately. Using a small offset spatula, spread the melted chocolate evenly over the toffee. Sprinkle the remaining ground hazelnuts over the chocolate in an even layer. Cool the toffee at room temperature for 10 minutes. Refrigerate for about 45 minutes, to set the chocolate.

Using the small offset spatula, lift up the toffee and break it into irregular pieces.

Serve the toffee at room temperature. Store the toffee between layers of wax paper in an airtight container at room temperature for 1 week or wrap the container with aluminum foil and store it in the refrigerator for up to 3 weeks or in the freezer for up to 2 months.

Makes about 30 pieces

Sesame Toffee Squares

GOLDEN BROWN SUGAR, BUTTER, AND CREAM ARE SOME
OF THE INGREDIENTS THAT MAKE UP THIS CHEWY CANDY.
THE SESAME SEEDS ADD NUTTY FLAVOR AND CRUNCH.

2 tablespoons unsalted butter, softened, for the baking sheet
8 tablespoons (1 stick) unsalted butter, cut into small pieces
¼ cup granulated sugar
¼ cup (firmly packed) golden brown sugar
2 tablespoons plus 1 teaspoon light corn syrup
2 tablespoons plus 1 teaspoon whipping cream
¼ cup sesame seeds

Coat the back of a baking sheet and the wheel of a pizza cutter with the 2 tablespoons of butter. Combine the 8 tablespoons of butter, the granulated sugar, brown sugar, corn syrup, and cream in a 2-quart heavy-bottomed saucepan. Cook over high heat, stirring constantly with a long-handled wooden spoon, until the mixture reaches 280°F. on a candy thermometer, about 8 minutes.

Remove the pan from the heat and quickly stir in the sesame seeds. Immediately turn the mixture out onto the prepared baking sheet and work quickly to spread it out to an 11 x 7-inch rectangle with the wooden spoon. Let stand for 3 minutes. Using the pizza wheel, cut the toffee into 1¼-inch squares while it is still warm. Let the toffee cool completely, about 30 minutes. Separate the cut pieces.

Serve the toffee at room temperature. Store the toffee between layers of wax paper in an airtight container at room temperature for up to 10 days.

Makes about 48 squares

chewy caramels and mouth**watering** fudge

Butterscotch Caramels

THESE CARAMELS ARE FIRM YET CHEWY WITH A DEEP UNDERTONE OF BUTTERSCOTCH.
TO MAKE THEM EVEN RICHER, ADD A CUP OF CHOPPED TOASTED NUTS
WHEN STIRRING IN THE VANILLA.

2 tablespoons vegetable oil, such as canola
½ pound (2 sticks) unsalted butter, cut into small pieces
1¾ cups (firmly packed) golden brown sugar
½ cup granulated sugar
¼ teaspoon salt
¼ cup dark corn syrup
½ cup light corn syrup
1 cup whipping cream
1 teaspoon vanilla extract

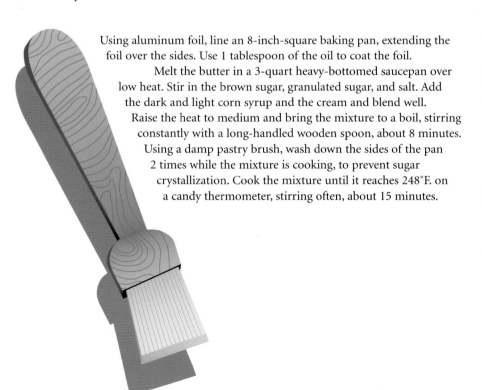

Using aluminum foil, line an 8-inch-square baking pan, extending the
foil over the sides. Use 1 tablespoon of the oil to coat the foil.
   Melt the butter in a 3-quart heavy-bottomed saucepan over
low heat. Stir in the brown sugar, granulated sugar, and salt. Add
the dark and light corn syrup and the cream and blend well.
   Raise the heat to medium and bring the mixture to a boil, stirring
constantly with a long-handled wooden spoon, about 8 minutes.
Using a damp pastry brush, wash down the sides of the pan
2 times while the mixture is cooking, to prevent sugar
crystallization. Cook the mixture until it reaches 248°F. on
a candy thermometer, stirring often, about 15 minutes.

Take the pan off the heat and quickly stir in the vanilla. Immediately turn the mixture out into the pan, making sure not to scrape out the bottom of the saucepan. Let stand at room temperature for 4 hours to set. Lift the candy from the pan by the foil, turn it out onto a cutting board, remove the foil, and turn it right side up. Coat a large chef's knife with the remaining tablespoon of vegetable oil and cut the caramels into eight 1-inch-wide strips, then cut each strip into 8 pieces.

Serve the caramels at room temperature. Store the caramels between layers of wax paper in an airtight container at room temperature for up to 10 days.

Makes 64 caramels

Creamy Caramels

THESE CANDIES CAN ONLY BE DESCRIBED AS THE ULTIMATE.
THEY ARE EVERYTHING A CARAMEL SHOULD BE—RICH, CREAMY, AND CHEWY.
IF YOU LIKE, ADD A CUP OF LIGHTLY CHOPPED TOASTED ALMONDS TO
THE MIXTURE JUST BEFORE IT IS TURNED INTO THE PAN TO SET.

2 tablespoons vegetable oil, such as canola
1½ cups sugar
¼ cup honey
½ cup light corn syrup
1½ cups whipping cream
1 vanilla bean, split lengthwise
2 tablespoons unsalted butter, softened

Using aluminum foil, line an 8-inch-square baking pan, extending the foil over the sides. Coat the foil generously with 1 tablespoon of the vegetable oil.

Combine the sugar, honey, and corn syrup in a 2-quart heavy-bottomed saucepan and bring to a boil over medium heat, stirring constantly with a long-handled wooden spoon. Using a damp pastry brush, wash down the sides of the pan 2 times while the mixture is cooking, to prevent sugar crystallization.

Increase the heat and cook the mixture until it reaches 305°F. on a candy thermometer. Meanwhile, in a separate saucepan, scald the cream with the vanilla bean over medium heat. Stir the butter into the caramel, 1 tablespoon at a time, while keeping the mixture boiling. Slowly stir the hot cream into the caramel and cook, stirring constantly, until the mixture reaches 250°F. about 15 minutes.

Take the pan off the heat, remove the vanilla bean with a fork, and turn the mixture out into the pan. Let stand at room temperature for 4 hours to set. Lift the candy from the pan by the foil, turn it out onto a cutting board, remove the foil, and turn the candy right side up. Coat a large chef's knife with the remaining vegetable oil, cut the caramels into eight 1-inch wide strips, then cut each strip into 8 pieces.

Serve the caramels at room temperature. Store the caramels between layers of wax paper in an airtight container at room temperature for up to 10 days.

Makes 64 caramels

Gingerbread Fudge

THE SAME INGREDIENTS THAT CREATE THE WARM, ROBUST FLAVOR OF GINGERBREAD ARE USED TO MAKE THIS UNUSUAL FUDGE.

3 tablespoons unsalted butter
1 cup superfine sugar
1 cup (firmly packed) golden brown sugar
¼ cup dark or robust-flavor molasses
¼ cup light corn syrup
½ cup whipping cream
Pinch of salt
½ teaspoon cream of tartar
2 tablespoons instant espresso powder dissolved in ¼ cup water
6 ounces bittersweet or semisweet chocolate, finely chopped
1 teaspoon vanilla extract
½ teaspoon ground cinnamon
¼ teaspoon ground ginger
¼ teaspoon ground cloves
¼ teaspoon freshly grated nutmeg

Using aluminum foil, line an 8-inch-square baking pan, extending the foil over the sides. Use 1 tablespoon of the butter to butter the foil. Rinse a jelly-roll pan with cold water, pour off the excess, and set the pan near the stove.

Combine the superfine sugar, brown sugar, molasses, corn syrup, cream, salt, cream of tartar, and espresso in a 3-quart heavy-bottomed saucepan over medium heat. Stir the mixture constantly with a long-handled wooden spoon to dissolve the sugar, 3 to 4 minutes. Using a damp pastry brush, wash down the sides of the pan 2 times while the mixture is cooking, to prevent crystallization.

Take the pan off the heat and stir in the chocolate in 3 to 4 batches until it is melted and smooth, 1 to 2 minutes. Return the pan to medium heat. Cook, without stirring, until the mixture reaches 238°F. on a candy thermometer, 20 to 25 minutes.

Take the pan off the heat and rapidly blend in the vanilla, the spices, and the remaining 2 tablespoons of butter. Stir the mixture briefly just to blend the ingredients and turn it out onto the jelly-roll pan. Leave the mixture to cool to 110°F. about 15 minutes.

Transfer the mixture to the bowl of a stand mixer or a mixing bowl. Using the flat beater attachment or a hand-held mixer, beat the mixture on low speed until it thickens, loses its sheen, and forms peaks, 5 to 10 minutes. Scrape down the sides of the bowl 2 or 3 times as it is beating.

Transfer the fudge to the pan. Using your fingertips, smooth the top and push the fudge into the corners. Let stand at room temperature for 1 to 2 hours to set. Lift the fudge from the pan by the foil. Cut the fudge into 6 rows each way.

Place each piece of fudge in a paper candy cup and serve at room temperature. Store the fudge between layers of wax paper in an airtight container at room temperature for up to 10 days.

Makes 36 pieces

Mocha-Spice Fudge

I CREATED THIS FUDGE FOR *BON APPETIT* MAGAZINE.
IT IS VERY RICH WITH DEEP UNDERTONES OF COFFEE AND CHOCOLATE.
IF YOU THINK YOU ARE NOT A FUDGE LOVER, TRY THIS AND THINK AGAIN.

2 tablespoons unsalted butter, softened
1 cup superfine sugar
1 cup (firmly packed) golden brown sugar
Pinch of salt
½ teaspoon cream of tartar
¼ cup light corn syrup
¾ cup whipping cream
3 tablespoons plus 1 teaspoon instant espresso powder dissolved in ¼ cup water
7 ounces bittersweet or semisweet chocolate, very finely chopped
½ teaspoon ground cinnamon
¼ teaspoon freshly grated nutmeg
1 teaspoon vanilla extract
1 cup roughly chopped walnuts
18 walnut halves cut in half lengthwise, for garnish

Using aluminum foil, line an 8-inch-square baking pan, extending the foil over the sides. Use ½ tablespoon of the butter to butter the foil. Cut the remaining 1½ tablespoons butter into small pieces and set aside. Rinse a jelly-roll pan with cold water, shake off the excess, and set the pan on the countertop near the stove.

Combine the superfine sugar, brown sugar, salt, cream of tartar, corn syrup, cream, and espresso in a 3-quart heavy-bottomed saucepan over medium heat. Stir the mixture constantly with a long-handled wooden spoon to dissolve the sugar, about 3 minutes. Using a damp pastry brush, wash down the sides of the pan 2 times while the mixture is cooking, to prevent sugar crystallization.

Take the pan off the heat and stir in the chocolate in 3 to 4 batches until it is melted and smooth, 1 to 2 minutes. Return the pan to medium heat. Cook, without stirring, until the mixture reaches 238°F. on a candy thermometer, 20 to 25 minutes.

Take the pan off the heat and immediately add the remaining 1½ tablespoons of butter, the spices, and vanilla. Stir the mixture quickly just to blend the ingredients. Turn it out onto the jelly-roll pan. Leave the mixture to cool to 110°F. about 15 minutes.

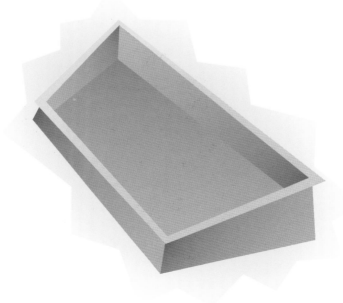

Transfer the mixture to the bowl of an electric mixer or a mixing bowl. Using the flat beater attachment or a hand-held mixer, beat the fudge on low speed until it thickens, loses its sheen, and forms peaks, 5 to 10 minutes. Scrape down the sides of the bowl 2 or 3 times as it is beating. Add the chopped walnuts and beat another minute or two, just to blend.

Transfer the fudge to the pan. Using your fingertips, smooth the top and push the fudge into the corners. Place the fudge on a cooling rack and let stand at room temperature for 1 to 2 hours to set.

Lift the fudge from the pan by the aluminum foil. Using a 1½-inch heart-shape cookie cutter, cut the fudge into pieces. Or cut the fudge into 6 rows each way. Place a walnut quarter diagonally in the center of each piece with its cut side down. Press lightly on the walnut so that it adheres. Vary the direction of the walnut pieces by placing one pointing to the upper left corner, then the next to the upper right corner.

Place each piece of fudge in a paper candy cup and serve at room temperature. Store the fudge between layers of wax paper in an airtight container at room temperature for up to 10 days.

Makes 25 fudge hearts or 36 fudge squares

felicitous
fruits

Apricot-Almond Balls

THESE CAN BE MADE TO LOOK LIKE THEY ARE THREE DIFFERENT CANDIES
DEPENDING ON WHETHER THEY ARE ROLLED IN SUPERFINE SUGAR,
FINE COCONUT, OR CONFECTIONERS' SUGAR.
THEY ARE GREAT TO MAKE WITH CHILDREN BECAUSE
AN EXTRA PAIR OF HANDS IS A BIG HELP AND
THERE IS NO COOKING INVOLVED.

½ cup dried apricots
⅓ cup whole unblanched almonds
½ cup unsweetened finely grated coconut
1 teaspoon finely minced lemon zest
1 teaspoon finely minced orange zest
¾ teaspoon freshly squeezed lemon juice
2½ teaspoons freshly squeezed orange juice
1 teaspoon amaretto, optional
2 tablespoons confectioners' sugar
¼ cup superfine sugar, for garnish
¼ cup unsweetened finely grated coconut, for garnish
¼ cup sifted confectioners' sugar, for garnish

Combine the apricots, almonds, the ½ cup of coconut, lemon and orange zest, lemon and orange juice, amaretto, and the 2 tablespoons of confectioners' sugar in the workbowl of a food processor fitted with a steel blade. Pulse until the mixture is very finely chopped and holds together, about 1½ minutes.

Place the superfine sugar, the ¼ cup of coconut, and the ¼ cup of confectioners' sugar in separate small bowls. Take a walnut-size piece of the apricot-almond mixture and shape it into a ball in your hands. Place the ball in one of the small bowls and toss it to coat it thoroughly. Remove the ball from the bowl and place it in a paper candy cup. Repeat with the rest of the mixture until it is all used.

Serve the balls at room temperature. Store the balls between layers of wax paper in an airtight container in the refrigerator for up to 3 weeks or in the freezer for up to 2 months.

Makes 24 balls

Walnut-stuffed Dates

IF YOU LIKE DATES, YOU'LL LOVE THESE CANDIES.
THEY ARE EASY-TO-MAKE AND DISAPPEAR FAST.

36 Deglet Noor or Empress dates, pitted
36 walnut halves
¾ cup superfine sugar

Split 1 side of each date open lengthwise. Fit a walnut half into the date and close it around the nut. Repeat. Place the superfine sugar in a shallow bowl. Place the stuffed dates, one at a time, in the superfine sugar and roll them around to coat completely.

Place the dates in paper candy cups and serve at room temperature. Store the dates between layers of wax paper in an airtight container in the refrigerator for up to 2 weeks.

Makes 36 stuffed dates

Variation:

COCONUT-ALMOND DATES

Replace each walnut half with 2 toasted unblanched almonds. Roll the stuffed dates in 1 cup finely grated coconut.

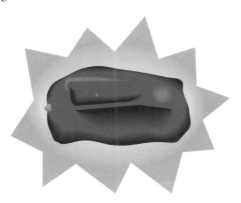

$\mathcal{D}$ate $\mathcal{N}$uggets

THESE CANDIES ARE GREAT TO HAVE ON HAND FOR
AFTER-SCHOOL OR AFTER-DINNER TREATS.

48 whole dates, pitted
2 teaspoons freshly squeezed orange juice or 2 teaspoons cognac or amaretto
⅔ cup toasted slivered almonds, finely chopped, or
⅔ cup unsweetened finely grated coconut, for garnish

Chop the dates into small pieces and place in the workbowl of a food processor fitted with a steel blade. Add the juice and pulse until the mixture is very finely chopped and holds together, about 1½ minutes.

Place the almonds or coconut in a small bowl. Pinch off walnut-size pieces of the date mixture and shape each into a ball in your hands. Place the balls, one at a time, in the bowl of almonds or coconut and toss to coat thoroughly.

Place the nuggets in paper candy cups and serve at room temperature. Store the nuggets between layers of wax paper in an airtight container in the refrigerator for up to 3 weeks or in the freezer for up to 2 months.

Makes about 40 nuggets

Candied Citrus Peel

I HAVE BEEN MAKING CANDIED CITRUS PEEL THIS WAY FOR THE PAST 20 YEARS.
IT IS SO MUCH BETTER THAN STORE-BOUGHT THAT ONCE YOU MAKE IT,
I DOUBT YOU'LL BUY IT AGAIN. IT IS USED TO MAKE NUMEROUS OTHER CANDIES.
SINCE IT KEEPS VERY WELL, YOU CAN ALWAYS HAVE IT ON HAND WHEN
THE CANDY-MAKING MOOD STRIKES. BE SURE TO CHOOSE FRUIT
WITH EVENLY COLORED, UNBLEMISHED SKIN.

4 large thick-skinned oranges, 6 lemons, 7 limes, 6 tangerines, or 2 grapefruits
3 cups sugar
2 tablespoons orange-flavored liqueur

Cut both ends off of the fruit, quarter the fruit, and cut off most of the pulp. Place the fruit in a 3-quart heavy-bottomed saucepan and fill with cold water. Bring to a boil over high heat and boil for 5 minutes. Strain the fruit and place it back in the saucepan. Fill with fresh cold water, bring to a boil over high heat, and boil for 5 minutes. Strain the fruit again, place it back in the saucepan, and again fill with fresh cold water. Bring to a boil over high heat and boil for 5 minutes.

Strain the fruit and refresh it under cold water. If any of the pulp is left, cut it off, and slice the peel ⅛-inch thick. Place the slices in the saucepan with 1½ cups of the sugar and the liqueur. Cook over low heat, stirring occasionally with a long-handled wooden spoon, to dissolve the sugar, about 5 minutes. Cook over low heat, stirring often, until there is no syrup remaining in the pan, about 1 hour.

Line 2 baking sheets with wax paper. Mound the remaining sugar on one of the baking sheets. Fill a large spoon with some of the fruit slices and place them on the sugar. Toss the fruit in the sugar, separating the individual slices and covering them completely with sugar. Place the sugar-covered slices on the other baking sheet. Leave them to air dry, about 30 minutes.

Serve the candied peel at room temperature. Store the peel between layers of wax paper in an airtight container in the refrigerator for up to 4 months.

Makes 3 cups candied peel

ingredients

START WITH THE VERY BEST INGREDIENTS AND you will end up with the best-tasting candy possible. The difference in cost between inferior and superior ingredients is often very small. ✳ Also, since few ingredients are used to make candy, it is hard to disguise second-rate ingredients.

$\mathcal{B}utter$

Always use unsalted butter, which has a much fresher and finer taste than salted butter. Using unsalted butter allows you to control how much salt, if any, goes into your candy. Because salt acts as a preservative, unsalted butter will not last as long as salted butter. Store unsalted butter in the freezer if you plan to keep it for more than a week. Most recipes call for butter to be at room temperature. If you use margarine or other butter substitutes for real butter, the candies will have a different taste.

$\mathcal{C}hocolate$

To choose chocolate, whether it is bittersweet, semisweet, milk, or white, taste it. Chocolate tastes the same whether it is plain, cooked, or baked. Don't expect the taste to change when you use it for making candies. Extra care has to be taken when choosing white chocolate. Some brands are very chalky tasting, while others are smooth and creamy. Be sure the white chocolate you use has cocoa butter as its base or it won't taste like chocolate.

    Bittersweet and semisweet chocolates, sometimes referred to as dark chocolates, can almost always be substituted for each other when making candy. Milk chocolate and white chocolate can't be substituted for each other or for bittersweet or semisweet chocolates because milk and white chocolates have less body than the dark chocolates. Baking chocolate squares are made from pure unsweetened chocolate. They work well for baking but are not suitable for use in candy recipes.

    For dipping candies it is best to use couverture chocolate, which is what is used by professionals. This chocolate has a higher percentage of cocoa butter than regular chocolate, which makes the chocolate thinner, resulting in a smooth, thin coating. Couverture chocolate can also be used for the candy centers and fillings. Couverture comes in bittersweet, semisweet, milk, and white chocolate and is available in many gourmet and cookware shops and through mail-order sources. (Regular chocolate is fine to use for dipping, but it will give a thicker coating than couverture.)

    The brands of both dark and white chocolate couverture that I recommend are Callebaut (Belgian), Cocoa Berry (French), Lindt (Swiss), Valrhona (French), and Hawaiian Vintage Chocolate (American—dark only). Guittard (American) and Ghirardelli (American), although not couvertures, also work well for candy making.

Store bulk chocolate at room temperature wrapped in aluminum foil. Don't use plastic wrap; it holds moisture. There is no need to store chocolate in the refrigerator or freezer. The condensation from the dampness will coat the chocolate. If water mixes with the melted chocolate, the chocolate will thicken and become difficult to work with. Dark chocolate, including couverture chocolate, can last practically forever if stored properly. Milk chocolate and white chocolate, because they contain milk solids, can normally be stored no longer than a year.

Chocolate should be chopped very fine for melting. Always melt it slowly in the top of a double boiler over hot water. Too much heat will cause chocolate to become grainy and seize up or thicken. Stir the chocolate often with a rubber or plastic spatula while it is melting. Be careful not to allow any water or liquid to come in contact with chocolate unless specifically called for in a recipe. A small amount of liquid will cause the chocolate to seize up, resembling mud. Make sure all utensils used with chocolate are dry; when the top of the double boiler is taken off of the water, dry the bottom and sides of the pan thoroughly.

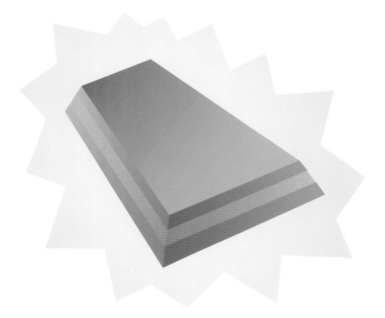

Many people recommend using a microwave oven to melt chocolate. I don't like to use this method because it is too easy to burn the chocolate. Because microwave melts from the inside out, it is difficult to tell if the chocolate is melted unless you stir it often. If you choose to melt your chocolate in a microwave oven, use low power for 15-second intervals and be sure to stir the chocolate at each break.

To give molded and dipped candies a smooth, even sheen, chocolate must be tempered. Tempered chocolate sets quickly, breaks cleanly, and slips out of molds without any problem because it contracts when cool. Cocoa butter, which is part of the cocoa bean, is a main component of chocolate. Tempering captures cocoa butter at its most stable point so it won't rise to the surface, causing unsightly white or gray streaks and dots. Chocolate leaves the factory tempered, but once it is heated, it goes out of temper and must be retempered if it is to be used for molding and dipping.

The process of tempering chocolate involves heating it to melt all the cocoa butter, cooling it, and heating it again to a specific temperature. Included are instructions for both the Classic Method and the Quick Method for tempering chocolate. The Classic Method is the more dependable method and lasts the longest. The Quick Method is easier and works well, but because the chocolate is not as stable, it will not last as long; up to 3 days, in most cases. When chocolate goes out of temper, gray or white streaks or dots appear on its surface, as a result of the cocoa butter breaking out of the emulsion and rising to the surface of the chocolate. These dots or streaks do not affect the taste of the chocolate, only its appearance.

Classic Method for Tempering Chocolate

Melt 1 pound of finely chopped chocolate in the top of a double boiler over hot water. Stir the chocolate often with a rubber spatula to help it melt evenly. When the chocolate is completely melted, take the double boiler off the heat, take off the top pan, and thoroughly wipe off the water. Cool the chocolate by stirring it for a minute or two. Pour two thirds of the chocolate out onto the center of a marble slab (page 113). Using an offset spatula (page 108), spread the chocolate out so that it covers most of the marble, then gather it back into a mound using a plastic pastry scraper. Do this 3 or 4 times. Take the chocolate's temperature with a chocolate or instant-read thermometer (page 106); it should read between 78° and 80°F.

 Put the chocolate back in the pan and stir it with the remaining chocolate until completely combined. This will take a few minutes. Take the temperature of the chocolate again. For dark chocolate the temperature range should be 88° to 91°F., for milk chocolate 85° to 88°F., and for white chocolate 84° to 87°F.

 If you find that the final temperature of the chocolate is a little low, put it back into the double boiler over low heat. If the temperature of the chocolate is too high, the chocolate has to be tempered again.

Quick Method for Tempering Chocolate

Finely chop 1 pound of chocolate. Place two thirds of the chocolate in the top of a double boiler over hot water. Stir the chocolate often with a rubber spatula to help it melt evenly. Take the double boiler off the heat, take off the top pan, and thoroughly wipe off the water. Blend in the remaining chocolate a tablespoon at a time. Be sure the chocolate has melted completely before adding any more. This added chocolate cools down the melted chocolate and brings it into temper. To test if the chocolate is at the correct temperature, place a dab under your lower lip. It should feel comfortable, not hot or cold. If it feels too warm, stir in 1 or 2 additional tablespoons of finely chopped chocolate to cool it down. If it feels too cool, put it back into the double boiler over low heat.

Whichever method you use to temper chocolate, the temperature of the tempered chocolate has to be kept constant while dipping candies. The best method for doing this is to have the water in the bottom pan 2°F. higher than the chocolate. To keep this water at an even temperature you'll need to change it occasionally. As an alternative, put the pan of tempered chocolate on a heating pad on a low setting.

Stir the chocolate often while working with it. If it clings to the sides of the pan it will become too cool and go out of temper. When dipping candies for more than half an hour you may need to retemper the chocolate.

Cocoa Powder

The best cocoa powder to use for candy is called Dutch process. Dutch process cocoa is not interchangeable with nonalkalized cocoa powder. Dutch process, developed in the early nineteenth century by the Dutch chemist, Coenraad van Houten, involves adding alkali to the cocoa powder during processing to reduce its natural acidity. This produces a richer, mellower, and more flavorful cocoa powder. All European cocoa powders are Dutch process. The label on a box or canister of cocoa powder usually states whether it is Dutch process. If not, it is possible to tell by the brand name of the cocoa. Van Houten and Droste are the most well known, widely available brands of Dutch process cocoa powder. Hershey calls its Dutch process cocoa European style.

Liqueurs

Liqueurs are often used to enhance the flavor of candies. Only a small amount is needed. Be sure to use the same quality that you would drink. Some of the most commonly used ones are port; dark rum; cognac; Grand Marnier, Cointreau, and curaçao (all orange); Chambord (black raspberry); kirschwasser (cherry); framboise (raspberry); Canton (ginger); Galliano (herbs and spices for a vanilla and anise flavor); Kahlúa (coffee); amaretto (almond); Frangelico (hazelnut); and Nocello (walnut). Many of these can be found in small individual serving bottles in liquor stores. Buying them this way gives you a chance to try them out before investing in a large bottle. Liqueurs are best stored in a cool, dry place, tightly capped to prevent excess evaporation.

$\mathcal{N}uts$

Nuts give both texture and flavor to candies. All nuts have a tendency to rancidity because of their high natural oil content. For this reason all nuts should be stored in the freezer. Keep nuts in airtight containers or in plastic bags; they will last for up to a year.

    The flavor of most nuts is intensified when they are toasted. Toast nuts by spreading them evenly on an ungreased baking sheet. Heat them in a preheated 350°F. oven, stirring every 5 minutes. Toast them until they are golden colored, about 15 minutes. Because sliced almonds are so thin they will need only about 6 minutes; stir them or shake the pan after 3 minutes. Remove the baking sheet from the oven and cool on a rack. To very lightly toast any nut, remove the pan from the oven after 6 minutes. For hazelnuts, after they have cooled for 10 minutes, rub them between your hands or in a towel to make most of the skins flake off.

    To grind nuts, place them in the workbowl of a food processor fitted with a steel blade. For each cup of nuts add 1½ tablespoons sugar to absorb the natural oil that is released during grinding. Process the nuts and sugar until finely ground, about 1 minute. Chop nuts either by hand with a chef's knife or in the workbowl of a food processor.

    Buy nuts from a store that has a high turnover to ensure that they are fresh. It's a good idea to keep your freezer stocked with a variety of nuts, so you have what you need on hand when you have the spontaneous impulse to make candy. Walnuts, almonds (whole unblanched, sliced, and slivered), hazelnuts, and pecans are the most commonly used nuts. Buy them shelled but raw, so you can toast them or not as needed for your recipes. Other nuts you may want to have on hand are pistachio nuts, pine nuts, and macadamia nuts.

Sugar and Other Sweeteners

Sugar sweetens candies and amplifies the flavor of other ingredients. Granulated sugar is the ubiquitous table sugar. Superfine sugar is more highly granulated than regular granulated sugar. It dissolves rapidly and leaves no grainy residue. Granulated and superfine sugar can be substituted for each other. Superfine sugar is available in many major supermarkets and large liquor stores, where it is sometimes called bar sugar. If you can't find it, you can easily make your own. Place granulated sugar in a blender or the workbowl of a food processor fitted with a steel blade and pulse for 30 seconds to 1 minute. Store sugar at room temperature in a tightly covered container.

Golden brown sugar.

ALSO CALLED LIGHT BROWN SUGAR. This sugar has molasses left in during the sugar refining process, which gives it a robust flavor. It tends to dry out quickly and harden when exposed to air for any length of time. Dark brown sugar has more molasses than golden brown sugar, which gives it a fuller, more pronounced flavor and imparts a darker color when it is used. Brown sugar needs to be tightly packed for measuring because the air trapped between its crystals must be pressed out to get a true measure. Store brown sugar in an airtight container at room temperature.

Confectioners' sugar.

ALSO CALLED POWDERED SUGAR. This is granulated sugar that has been ground to a powder and mixed with a little cornstarch. It dissolves easily and should always be sifted.

Liquid sweeteners.

CORN SYRUP, HONEY, AND MOLASSES are all used in candy making. Corn syrup is used to sweeten candies. Because it naturally attracts moisture, one of its main roles is to prevent sugar from becoming grainy when it is cooking. Corn syrup is available in light and dark styles. The two are not usually substituted for each other because of their different flavors. Once opened, store corn syrup tightly capped in the refrigerator.

Honey sweetens candies and adds texture. Like corn syrup, honey naturally attracts moisture and helps to prevent sugar crystallization. Honey itself may crystallize with age. To bring it back to liquid simply heat the jar slowly in a pan of water or warm it in a microwave oven on low power. Store honey tightly capped in a cool, dry place.

Molasses is the liquid left after sugar crystals are removed during the sugar refining process. This liquid is then boiled down to various grades. Light molasses comes from the first boiling, dark from the second, and blackstrap from the third. Dark molasses is the type used most often in candy making. It is sometimes labeled robust-flavor. Occasionally molasses is processed with sulphur dioxide. If so, the label on the jar will state this. All types of molasses have a distinct, rich flavor. It primarily adds sweetness and moisture to candies. Molasses is available in most supermarkets and health-food stores. Store opened molasses tightly capped in the refrigerator.

tools of the trade

You PROBABLY ALREADY
have most of what you
need to make
candy. However,
if you do need to buy
something, the best places
to look are cookware shops, candy
making and cake decorating supply shops,
the cookware sections of major department stores,
and most large supermarkets.

Double Boiler

To melt chocolate without burning it, a
double boiler must be used. Make sure
the top pan fits snugly over the bottom
pan so no water or steam can escape.
A glass double boiler allows you
to see the water in the bottom pan
so you can tell if it is getting too hot.
A double boiler can be improvised
with any saucepan and a snug-fitting
bowl. Be sure to use a double boiler that is
large enough to hold the amount of chocolate
you want to melt and allows room for stirring.

Thermometers

A mercury candy thermometer, designed to read in 2-degree
increments in the range of 100° to 400°F., is a very important
tool for candy making. To make sure your thermometer
is accurate, place it in a pan of boiling water. The
thermometer should read 212°F. If it is off by a degree
or two, make the necessary adjustment in the
recipe temperature when using the thermometer.
For a correct temperature reading, read the
thermometer at eye level.

Thermometers designed solely for chocolate are long glass tubes that enclose a center tube of mercury. These thermometers read in the range of 40° to 130°F. and are designed to read in 1-degree increments. They are extremely accurate, which is vital to chocolate work. Instant-read thermometers with a range of 0° to 140° or 220° F. are also good for chocolate work. A meat thermometer is not acceptable for candy and chocolate work because it does not register in the correct temperature ranges.

Thermometers are fragile and should be handled with extreme care. Wash and dry them by hand and store them away from other utensils.

Candy and Truffle Dippers

These are hand tools made to hold candies and truffles when dipping them into chocolate. The European-made dippers have a wooden handle with a firm metal wire extension. American-made dippers use a single piece of plastic. Both styles come with a special shape on one end for picking up candy. Shapes used include oval, round, spiral, and forks with different numbers of prongs. You can make your own candy and truffle dippers from plastic forks by simply breaking out the 2 middle tines.

Offset Spatula

This kind of spatula has a stainless-steel, flexible blade with straight sides and a round tip attached to a wooden handle. The blade has a 1-inch downward bend or angle near the handle so that your hand stays above the surface you are working on. A 10- to 12-inch blade is used primarily for tempering chocolate. A 4-inch blade has many functional and decorative uses for candy making.

Rubber Spatulas

Rubber spatulas are ideal for stirring chocolate because they don't absorb other flavors like wooden utensils. The blade on a rubber spatula is straight on both sides with a well-rounded curve on one side of the tip, which makes it easy to get into small spaces. Small spatulas (9¼ inches long) are used mostly in candy making. Rubber spatulas can be cleaned in the dishwasher.

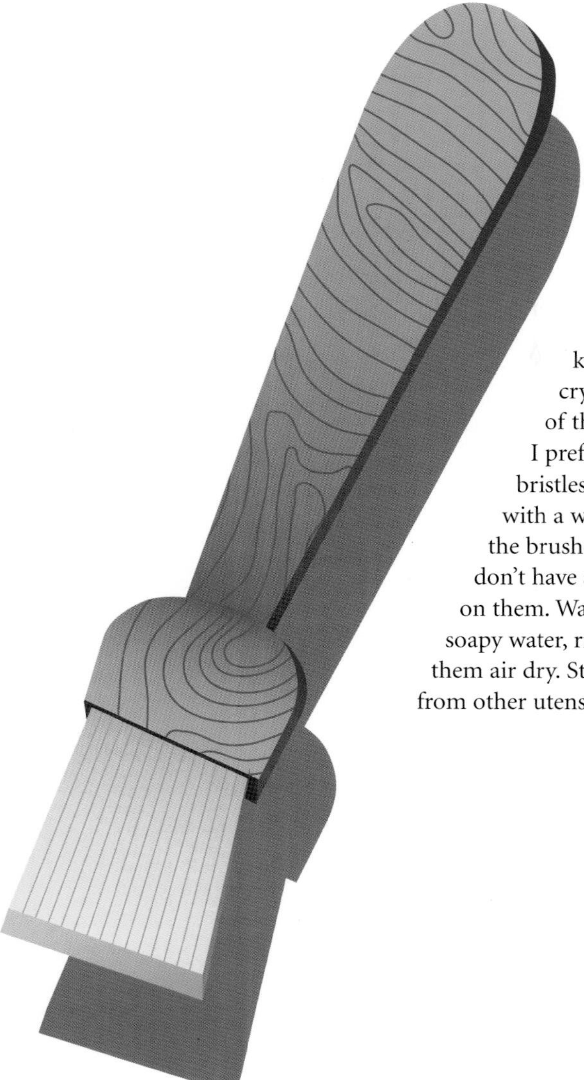

Pastry Brushes

In candy making,
these are used
primarily to wash
down the inside of a
saucepan while a sugar
mixture is cooking, to
keep the sugar from
crystallizing on the sides
of the pan. The brushes
I prefer to use have natural
bristles. They are 1 inch wide
with a wooden handle. Be sure
the brushes used for sugar mixtures
don't have any grease or other material
on them. Wash your brushes with warm
soapy water, rinse thoroughly, and let
them air dry. Store them separately
from other utensils.

Pastry Bags and Tips

I prefer to use pastry bags made of nylon or soft polyester fabric, because they are lightweight and easy to wash. Twelve or 14-inch pastry bags are best because they are large enough to hold a mixture yet leave room for handling. In order for the pastry tip to fit comfortably in a new pastry bag, cut off about ½-inch of the pointed end.

      Large, 2-inch-high pastry tips are preferable. Plain round tips with about a ½-inch opening (numbers 4, 5, and 6) are best for piping out truffle mixtures; closed star tips (numbers 3 and 4) are best for making swirled designs. The numbers are plainly marked on the front of the tips.

To fit the bag with the tip, drop the tip with its tapered end down, into the bag. To fill a pastry bag, fold over the top edge about 2 to 3 inches to form a cuff. Hold the bag underneath the cuff or stand the bag upright in a tall glass jar. Fill the bag no more than halfway, then unfold the cuff. Holding the pastry bag by the top end, push the filling down toward the tip and twist the bag tightly at the point where the filling stops. To refill the bag, repeat the process.

Parchment Paper Pastry Bags

These can also be made out of parchment paper triangles. The triangles can be bought already cut or you can cut your own. The best size is 12 x 12 x 15 inches. To make a cone out of the triangle, hold it away from you with the long side up. Bend the right point into the center so that it lines up with the point at the bottom; clasp these points between the thumb and forefinger of your right hand. Wrap the left point of the triangle so that it comes around the front counter clockwise and lines up with the other points to form a cone. If necessary, manipulate the ends so the pointed end of the cone is completely closed. Fold the 3 points into the cone twice to make an even edge. Use a rubber spatula to place a mixture into the cone, making sure not to fill it more than halfway. Fold the sides of the cone into the center, then fold the top down so it secures the filling. Use scissors to snip off the pointed end. Start with a small opening; you can always cut a larger one if necessary. If you are using a pastry tip with the cone, cut the opening and place the tip in the cone before the filling. Once used, parchment paper cones cannot be refilled; they must be discarded.

Baking Sheets and Pans

Even though there is no baking involved in candy making, many of the recipes call for a mixture to be piped out or turned out onto a baking sheet or pan. I use jelly-roll pans (baking sheets that have a 1-inch high lip around the outer edge) almost exclusively, but any baking pan or cookie sheet will do. Since it's not going in the oven, there's no need to be concerned about quality. I always recommend lining the pans with wax paper, which makes clean-up a breeze. For toasting a small quantity of nuts or coconut, I usually use a round cake pan or pie plate made of heavy aluminum or glass because they conduct heat well.

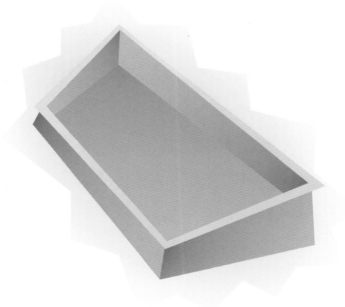

Scale

An accurate kitchen scale is necessary if you buy bulk chocolate and chop it yourself. Either a spring, a balance, or an electronic scale can be used; just be sure it is accurate. I use a spring scale that has a removable bowl. That way, I can use different bowls or containers for measuring. I am also able to adjust the dial to zero to ensure an accurate measurement with whatever size bowl I use. Scales are available at most cookware shops.

Marble Slabs and Rolling Pins

Although not absolutely necessary, a good-quality marble slab is ideal for tempering chocolate. Many cookware shops and mail-order catalogs carry good size square or rectangle marble slabs. A slab that measures 18 x 24 x ¾ inch is a good size. If it is any bigger, it will be too heavy to move. Never use your marble slab as a cutting board. It will dull knives and the knife cuts will cause the chocolate to stick to the marble.

Marble rolling pins are ideal for rolling out hot brittle mixtures, such as Hazelnut-Almond Brittle (page 71), because the marble won't stick to the brittle. A good alternative to marble is a heavy metal or copper-covered rolling pin.

Chocolate Molds

There is an almost unlimited variety of chocolate molds available in cookware and candy making supply shops. The transparent plastic molds are the best to use because they are flexible, allowing the chocolate to be released easily. Make sure the cavities of the molds are not scratched or the chocolate will stick to them. Treat the molds with care, wash them with warm soapy water, and don't use any abrasive, which will scratch the molds. Dry them with a soft towel. Make sure they are completely dry before use.

Dredger

A dredger is a cylinder slightly smaller than a 1-cup measure. Plastic dredgers have a half-moon shape mesh plastic or metal screen on top. Metal dredgers have a flat perforated top. Both types have a handle attached to the side and the tops are removable. A dredger is used to hold confectioners' sugar or cocoa powder. As the sugar or cocoa is shaken from the dredger, it is sifted through the top.

Paper and Foil Candy Cups

These are used to hold candies so they can be handled easily without picking up fingerprints. Candy cups with fluted edges are the most popular. They measure 1½ x ⅝ inches. To prevent the candy cups from absorbing moisture from the candies, use glassine cups. Various colors are available.

Liquid candy mixtures or soft truffle creams can be piped into fluted-edge foil candy cups. These cups imprint a fluted design in the sides of the candy. They are small, measuring 1 x ⅝ inch and are available in gold, red, and green.

Serving, Storing, and Packaging

All candies taste best at room temperature. Candies can be presented several ways; on colorful plates or unusually shaped dishes or in interesting containers, like baskets and trays. Almost anything goes—just let your imagination be your guide.

Truffles and most chocolate candies are best stored in the refrigerator between layers of wax paper in an airtight container. Be sure to use a few layers of aluminum foil to wrap the containers and place them away from most other food. Take them out of the refrigerator at least 1 hour before serving so they can develop their full flavor.

Truffles and chocolate candies can be frozen. Again, wrap the container in several layers of foil. Defrost the candies slowly by letting them stand in the refrigerator for a minimum of 24 hours. The outer chocolate coating on the candies will discolor and may crack if it undergoes quick changes in temperature.

Brittles, toffee, caramels, and fudge are best stored between layers of wax paper in airtight containers at room temperature. If refrigerated they will pick up too much moisture and become soft and crumbly. In general, it is best to pack your candies no more than 3 layers deep so they don't get crushed.

Using colorful and unusual tins and paper boxes is an appealing way to package your candies for gifts. Tins protect candies that are sent through the mail. Keep your eyes open for tins and boxes in cookware shops, gift and card stores, art supply stores, antique stores, and shops that specialize in coffee and tea and other gourmet items. Pack the candies between layers of wax paper and include a note telling the recipient how to serve and store them.

mail-order sources

Bridge Kitchenware
214 East 52nd Street
New York, NY 10022
(212) 688-4220
EQUIPMENT AND TOOLS

J. B. Prince Company
29 West 38th Street
New York, NY 10018
(212) 302-8611
EQUIPMENT AND TOOLS

Kitchen Witch Gourmet Shop
127 N. El Camino Real, Suite D
Encinitas, CA 92024
(619) 942-3228
EQUIPMENT AND INGREDIENTS

La Cuisine
323 Cameron Street
Alexandria, VA 22314
(800) 521-1176
EQUIPMENT AND INGREDIENTS

Maid of Scandinavia
3244 Raleigh Avenue
Minneapolis, MN 55416
(800) 328-6722
EQUIPMENT AND INGREDIENTS

Parish's Cake Decorating Supplies
225 W. 146th Street
Gardena, CA 90248
(800) 736-8443
EQUIPMENT AND TOOLS

Williams-Sonoma
Mail Order Department
P.O. Box 7456
San Francisco, CA 94120-7456
(800) 541-2233
EQUIPMENT AND INGREDIENTS

Wilton Industries, Inc.
2240 West 75th Street
Woodridge, IL 60517
(800) 772-7111
EQUIPMENT AND TOOLS

index

index

table of equivalents

THE EXACT EQUIVALENTS IN THE FOLLOWING TABLES
HAVE BEEN ROUNDED FOR CONVENIENCE.

US/UK
OZ=OUNCE
LB=POUND
IN=INCH
FT=FOOT
TBL=TABLESPOON
FL OZ=FLUID OUNCE
QT=QUART

METRIC
G=GRAM
KG=KILOGRAM
MM=MILLIMETER
CM=CENTIMETER
ML=MILLILITER
L=LITER

WEIGHTS

US/UK	METRIC
1 OZ	30 G
2 OZ	60 G
3 OZ	90 G
4 OZ (¼ LB)	125 G
5 OZ (⅓ LB)	155 G
6 OZ	185 G
7 OZ	220 G
8 OZ (½ LB)	250 G
10 OZ	315 G
12 OZ (¾ LB)	375 G
14 OZ	440 G
16 OZ (1 LB)	500 G
1 ½ LB	750 G
2 LB	1 KG
3 LB	1.5 KG

LENGTH MEASURES

⅛ IN	3 MM
¼ IN	6 MM
½ IN	12 MM
1 IN	2.5 CM
2 IN	5 CM
3 IN	7.5 CM
4 IN	10 CM
5 IN	13 CM
6 IN	15 CM
7 IN	18 CM
8 IN	20 CM
9 IN	23 CM
10 IN	25 CM
11 IN	28 CM
12/1 FT	30 CM

LIQUIDS

US	METRIC	UK
2 TBL	30 ML	1 FL OZ
¼ CUP	60 ML	2 FL OZ
⅓ CUP	80 ML	3 FL OZ
½ CUP	125 ML	4 FL OZ
⅔ CUP	160 ML	5 FL OZ
¾ CUP	180 ML	6 FL OZ
1 CUP	250 ML	8 FL OZ
1½ CUPS	375 ML	12 FL OZ
2 CUPS	1 L	32 FL OZ

OVEN TEMPERATURES

FAHRENHEIT	CELSIUS	GAS
250	120	½
275	140	1
300	150	2
325	160	3
350	180	4
375	190	5
400	200	6
425	220	7
450	230	8
475	240	9
500	260	10